D1570442

"Bob Fischer provides a wonderful new perspective into statistical prediction and investor psychology. I found this book to be a highly informative, readable, and noteworthy how-to guide of investing."

Victor Ricciardi, Editor,
Social Science Research Network Behavioral &
Experimental Finance eJournal
Lexington, Kentucky

"Fischer's book makes a good case for adopting a systematic approach as a way to maintain a disciplined and transparent investment process. Fischer outlines how innate human biases can cloud our judgment, and how a rule-based investment method can prevent us from falling victim to our own emotional shortcomings. The rules he proposes are value-based and founded on empirical research."

Taher Khan, Senior Quantitative Portfolio Manager,
Millennium Global Investments
London, England

"Fischer has firmly established himself as a thought leader in the rules-based investing realm. His breakthrough approach has enabled him to write a compelling finance book with no math. Very impressive. Hats off to Mr. Fischer!"

Thomas B. Scott, PhD, Quantitative Analysis
Business Department Chair
Sweet Briar College
Sweet Briar, Virginia

"Mr. Fischer has written an important book, one significant for more than his sound investment strategies. By identifying the ways smart people make the same mistakes over and over, he helps us steer a course of prudent and rewarding investing, using a system equally valuable to evidence-based medicine and rules-based law. The self-styled experts with pretentions of superior judgment, claims of vast experience, and assertions of prior success are supplanted with statistical prediction methods that Fischer wisely recommends because they are scrubbed clean of the biases inherent in an 'I'm smarter than you!' system."

Robert Hall, Attorney Hall and Sickles
Reston, Virginia

"Bob Fischer had me hooked at the title of this book. What a surprise to see the word *Naked* in the title of a book about investing methodologies. Nevertheless, I wondered whether the book would keep this rather ordinary person engaged. I'm glad I read on because I was occasionally entertained and always educated from the first page to the last.

One of Fischer's goals was to provide an easy-to-read tool to clients about the fundamentals of how their portfolios were invested and to explain his methodologies. The book is full of examples of how we mere mortals use information that we believe is reliable, only to be proven wrong. Fischer draws from his expertise as a chess master to illustrate the intricate and often mistaken ways in which the human brain reasons and reaches conclusions. Bob Fischer has written a book that sheds light on the often-mysterious process of statistical prediction methods by making portfolio management naked."

Sandra M. Rohrstaff
Attorney, Weiner Rohrstaff and Spivey
President, Virginia Trial Lawyers Association

"In *The Naked Portfolio Manager,* Bob Fischer takes a simple, yet innovative approach to the complicated issue of investing. He introduces and explains application of a method with proven results to an area known for its uncertain outcomes.

Bob uses evidence based methods as a tool in the practical approach towards investing. He bridges the gap between complex quantitative statistical methods and human judgment resulting from the advice from various sources.

Bob explains a strategy that results in less stress on one's nervous system. Less stress decreases the probability of panicked behavior during periods of unforeseen underperformance of stocks. This leads to better overall results and fewer serious errors occurring from abrupt change of strategy."

Michelle Mudge-Riley, DO, MHA
Director of Health Promotion and Wellness
Managed Benefits, Inc; Integrate Health For Results
Richmond, Virginia

THE
NAKED
PORTFOLIO MANAGER

THE
NAKED
PORTFOLIO MANAGER

WHY RULES TRUMP REASON
ON WALL STREET

ROBERT J. FISCHER, CFP

Bon Air, VA

The Naked Portfolio Manager

Abbalucci Press
2711 Buford Rd. #307
Bon Air, VA

Copyright © 2009 Robert J. Fischer

All rights reserved. No part of this book may be reproduced or transmitted in any form or by any means, electronic or mechanical, including photocopying, recording, or by any information storage and retrieval system, except in the case of brief quotation embodied in critical articles and reviews, without prior written permission of the publisher. For information, address all inquiries to Abbalucci Press.

Although the author and publisher have made every effort to ensure the accuracy and completeness of information contained in this book, we assume no responsibility for errors, inaccuracies, omissions, or any inconsistency herein. Any slights of people, places, or organizations are unintentional.

Printed in the United States of America

Publisher's Cataloging-in-Publication

Fischer, Robert J. (Robert Joseph)

The naked portfolio manager : why rules trump reason on Wall Street / Robert J. Fischer. — 1st ed. — Bon Air, VA : Abbalucci Press, c2009.

p. ; cm.
ISBN: 978-0-9840894-3-7
Includes bibliographical references and index.

1. Portfolio management—Statistical methods. 2. Investment analysis—Statistical methods. 3. Investment advisors—Handbooks, manuals, etc. I. Title.

HG4529.5 .F57 2009   2009905358
332.678--dc22   0908

Author Photo: Shawn Stanley
Illustrations: Carolyn Schallmo
Book Consultant: Ellen Reid
Book Design: Pamela Terry

This book is dedicated to a very special group of people who I call my clients. You are the people who have had faith in me, trusted me, encouraged me, and on occasion forgiven me. Other than immediate family, you are the most important people in my life. Whatever professional success I have achieved, I owe to you.

I love each and every one of you.

Contents

Foreword

I have known Bob Fischer for almost thirty years. From his days as my classmate at the United States Military Academy, he was taught to lead and improve processes. As part of his West Point training, he spent countless hours analyzing information, assessing situations, setting goals, and achieving successful outcomes.

But he was always questioning the status quo, fervently seeking new ideas and new approaches, and I was not surprised when he told me he had written a book recommending a new approach for making investment decisions.

I was intrigued too, as the topic of statistical prediction methods resonated with my own professional experience.

In fields such as medicine, evidence-based statistical decision-making algorithms are now routine. No longer are clinical decisions made from a black box of privileged information that was unavailable to the general public and, in many instances, unavailable to physicians.

This evidence-based approach, however, transcends medicine and serves as a model for change in many areas. It uncovers new truths that may be used to make future decisions.

Robert Fischer is using this approach to introduce a new way of investing. Through his extensive training and experiences, he has developed a model for navigating a very confusing landscape for many investors.

His lifelong quest for new ideas and new approaches has resulted in this new, evidence-based strategy for investment decision making.

Anthony Macchiavelli, MD
Medical Director, Associates in Hospitalist Medicine
Jefferson University Hospitals
Methodist Hospital
Philadelphia, PA

Acknowledgments

There are many people whom I need to thank for their help in putting this book together. While many people assisted me, there were four individuals whose contributions made this a substantially better work.

I especially want to thank Richard Cripps, CFA, a colleague who works as senior managing director at a regional brokerage house. Richard is blessed with a mind that allows him to think on a level different from most investment professionals. He was a very enthusiastic supporter of the book from the very beginning. Conversations with Richard helped formulate many of the key concepts and their examples.

Next I would like to thank Carolyn Schallmo, who illustrated the book. Carolyn's contribution to the book is substantial. Her illustrations drive home the essential message of the book in a way that is both memorable and entertaining. If you understand her pictures, you understand the fundamental truth of the book.

It is impossible to overstate the importance of Patrick Morin's contribution to this work. Patrick is a professional speaker with a unique gift for translating the abstract into concrete terms. He is the most enthusiastic and creative person I have ever known. At times his enthusiasm for the project exceeded even my own. He devoted countless hours to reading and improving the manuscript as well as developing concepts that Carolyn illustrated. He helped me through writer's block, acted as a sounding board for ideas, and constantly encouraged me.

Finally, I have to thank my editor, Deborah Nason. Every writer should be so lucky to have his editor understand the importance of his book, and I was very fortunate that Deborah, like Richard, Carolyn, and Patrick, developed great enthusiasm for the book and its message. She took a long and sometimes disjointed manuscript and carefully molded it, removing the unnecessary and shaping the text, to deliver the message with clarity and economy. Deborah was a demanding editor and at several points urged me to add content or find additional support for my ideas. Her work dramatically improved the manuscript.

Although he was not involved in the writing of the book, I must also acknowledge the contribution of International Grandmaster Gregory Kaidanov. Grandmaster Kaidanov showed me how chess players repeatedly make the same types of systemic thinking errors when deciding on a move. By extension, I was able to deduce that systemic thinking errors occurred in other fields of decision making under uncertainty, including portfolio management.

Besides my four main contributors and Grandmaster Kaidanov, there were many other people who helped me at various points in the book's creation. I would like to thank James B. Cloonan, President of the American Association of Individual Investors, and Professor Robyn Dawes of Carnegie Mellon University, who read the original manuscript and provided helpful feedback. Dr. Brendan Reilly of Cook County Hospital in Chicago provided important clarification for one of the key examples in the book. Tim McCann and Michael Scherer, analysts with a regional brokerage firm, and Otto Voit, the CFO of Keystone Industries, also provided valuable input.

Finally, I must thank Ellen Reid and her very talented team of writers, copy editors, and book designers who all came together to turn this manuscript into a book. Ellen never had a more difficult client, but she kept a positive attitude during the entire time we were putting the book together and ultimately made the book as good as it could be. Special thanks go to Pam Terry who I nearly drove to distraction insisting that the cover must be worthy of the book's message. In the end, we got it right.

Preface

My motivation for writing this book has changed.
Initially I intended only to write a book that would explain to clients how I manage money. But now that the book is finished, I realize it can serve a higher purpose. The reason I am so passionate about this book is that its message is fundamentally important for all investors.

Simply stated: **statistical prediction methodology is a superior way to make investment decisions.**

There are many well-meaning people who are well compensated for urging investors to use traditional methods—methods by which a human portfolio manager applies his training and experience to select what he believes are the best stocks for your portfolio. Yet when you review the record, individual investors' behavior combined with traditional methods of managing money have resulted in dismal performance. For example, the average equity fund investor has trailed the market by 8 percent a year. Consider that from 1986 through 2006, the S&P 500 averaged 11.9 percent while the average equity fund investor earned a paltry 3.9 percent.[1]

Yet despite the dismal record, fund companies and investors continue to follow the same old failed methods. Fund companies continue to introduce new traditionally managed fund offerings, and individual investors continue to make poor market timing decisions. Most equity funds trail their indexes, and a study of the two hundred most popular investment funds from 1996 through 2000 showed that in only two funds did the investors do as well as the fund.[2]

❏   ❏   ❏

I wrote this book for three reasons.
First, I needed a simple, easy-to-read tool to teach my clients how this fundamental truth applies to their portfolios and to explain my methodologies.

I consider one of my principal roles as an advisor to help my clients stay on course and avoid getting sidetracked by market noise. I know the din is relentless. They read and hear a tremendous amount of noise about how they should invest. Whether it comes from a co-worker at the water cooler, across the tennis court, from the financial tabloids, or from the talking heads on television, stock market noise can sidetrack clients and prevent them from following through with sound strategies.

Therefore, I wanted my clients to be able to pull this book down from their bookcases and reread some of the key chapters. The more tools I have to keep my clients following proven principles, the better I am able to keep them on the right track.

Second, I wrote this book for clients of other investment firms who needed a tool for assessing an existing or prospective advisor relationship. I believe the book serves as an exemplar of how an advisor should approach the business of making money for clients.

There are many good ways to invest but many more ways that are simply not effective. When considering working with an advisor, prospective clients should ask questions such as, "How do you make money for your clients?" and "What is your investment philosophy?" and "What is the evidence that your particular investment approach works over meaningful periods of time?" I will answer these questions in this book.

Investors should receive succinct, concise answers to these questions and avoid advisors who answer them in a vague or convoluted manner.

Third, I wrote this book to help fill a void in the literature on stock market investing. Casino gamblers know the odds and the risk-to-reward ratio before they make bets, but human judges frequently find themselves making decisions when they know neither the exact odds nor the range of possible results. A patient considering an operation has a range of results that will vary from being completely cured to death. We call decisions where the exact odds and risks and rewards are unknown decisions made *under uncertainty*. While there is a tremendous body of data about how people make decisions under uncertainty, there is a scarcity of literature that links the psychological research on decision making with the errors that individuals and professional investors make.

This book summarizes in layperson's terms much of what we know about the flaws in human decision making without the complex mathematical formulas often included in the scholarly works on human psychology.

More important, it provides practical approaches to investing, designed to capitalize on opportunities created by other investors' mistakes, and includes ways to avoid those mistakes yourself.

As you will read, almost two hundred studies have been conducted in diverse fields on how humans make decisions under uncertainty. In almost all, results showed statistical prediction methods to be superior to traditional human judgment. It is time to apply what we have learned about human decision making to the stock market.

PART I

The Case for
Statistical Decision Making

Introduction:
Looking Inside the Box

The traditional approach to marketing money management is to tell the investing public about the special powers of the portfolio manager.

Portfolio managers, we are told, are brilliant people who graduated at the tops of their classes in business school and use their unique intellect to divine the very best stock investments for your portfolio. We understand that they work tirelessly—sixty and seventy hours a week—to research the best investment ideas.

Individual investors, we are further told, simply do not have the training, experience, and resources to do what portfolio managers do. Sometimes we are led to believe that the portfolio manager has some sort of "black box" filled with secret proprietary research tools that allow him to identify winning stocks.

You, the investor, are not allowed to look inside the black box, but you wouldn't understand it anyway since what goes on in the box is very complicated and only the portfolio manager understands it. With some portfolio managers, the black box is in their heads and the stock picks they make come from a process that you could not possibly replicate since you can't think like the portfolio managers. Since you can't do what the portfolio manager does, the next best thing you can do is hire him to manage an account for you or buy his mutual fund.

Today there is a very small but growing number of portfolio managers who reject the traditional manager's premise. They do not have a black box. They have a clear box, and they will let you see what is inside. Even better, if you don't understand the inner workings of the box, they will explain it to you, as it is really not all that complicated.

These portfolio managers do not ask you to invest with them based on their "special powers" because, as they will freely admit, they have none. They will tell you that, once you understand the workings of the box, you can manage money just as well as they can. You might still want to hire them for a variety of reasons, however, even after you understand the workings of the box.

They understand this, which is why they are so forthcoming about their process. I call these advisors "naked portfolio managers" because they are completely exposed and their process is completely transparent.

So which type of advisor gives the investor the best chance of success? To answer that question, you need to understand a fundamental stock market truth, one that is fully understood by only a very few people on Wall Street: **It is the process that matters.**

If you understand this truth and arrange your investments to comply with its principles, it can give you a meaningful edge. There is no magic formula that works all the time or for all your stock purchases. By following the advice in this book, you might still buy stocks that go down and sell stocks and watch them go higher afterward.

This book will show you how to tilt the odds in your favor just slightly. And while the edge this truth can give you is small and difficult to measure in the short term, over a lifetime of investing, the advantage it will give you can have a very meaningful impact on your ability to accumulate wealth.

Deciding How to Decide

When approaching the problem of how to invest, most people have skipped the step of asking exactly how they should make decisions.

The majority of investors take one of two approaches when deciding how to invest:

1. In the first approach, they decide to buy stocks or bonds based on research they receive from their broker or find on their own. Some investors rely heavily on their brokers' advice, while others use their brokers only as information sources and to execute transactions. But regardless of how much they rely on their brokers' advice, these clients are making all the investment decisions themselves.

2. In the second approach, the investor decides to defer the selection of securities to a professional investor through a managed account or mutual fund. In this case the client pays a fee to the manager to exercise his judgment and select securities for the client.

My experience has shown that both of these approaches to investing are suboptimal.

The first decision should be not to buy stocks or pick managers, but to select a winning strategy and a method of implementing that strategy. The strategy, in turn, will determine what stocks are selected. The tool we recommend in our practice is the statistical model, or *algorithm*. Basically we establish a set of rules we believe will facilitate the construction of a winning portfolio, and we consistently follow those rules.

When an individual or portfolio manager selects stocks, he or she analyzes the available information then makes a decision to buy or sell a stock.

In our approach, however, data is combined and analyzed statistically, and the stocks are selected based on rules or numerical values.

In the first method, human judgment is used to select stocks. But in our method, human judgment is used to select rules and construct models, not select individual securities. Naked portfolio managers thus focus their energy on selecting effective rules and let the rules create the portfolio.

We will compare the following two methods of decision making in this book:

1. The first method is known as **clinical (or judgment-based) decision making.** For example, if a portfolio manager analyzes earnings trends, studies industry reports, reviews price action charts, and makes his decision in his head based on his experience, knowledge, or intuition, he is using *clinical* judgment. It is very important to remember that clinical decision making does not mean decisions made by a clinician or someone who works in a clinic. If the decision maker is combining facts in his head to make the decision, he is using clinical decision making.

2. In the second method, known as actuarial or **statistical decision making,** once the data is combined, no special expertise is necessary to make a decision. For example, if a portfolio manager takes the available data and puts it into a spreadsheet and calculates a score for each of the companies he is considering, he is combining the data statistically. If he can ask a person not trained in his field, such as his secretary, wife, nine-year-old daughter, or personal trainer, to pick the stock with the highest score and they

all pick the same stock, he is using actuarial or statistical decision making.

For the purposes of our discussion, we will use the term **statistical prediction method,** or **SPM,** to describe the second method, regardless of whether the decision-making tool is a table, spreadsheet, or algorithm. Also, while we realize that the term for the decision maker who bases his decisions on experience or intuition is "clinical decision maker," in the text we have chosen to call this person "the human judge" or simply "the judge." We think that for the ordinary investor, the term *judge* is much more descriptive and an easier term to use.

❑   ❑   ❑

We realize that human judges frequently incorporate statistics into their decision making. Therefore, it is very important to distinguish between a judgment-based method that uses statistics and a statistical decision-making method.

If a decision employs statistical data so a layperson can look at the data and make the same decision as an expert would, then statistical decision making is taking place.

If, after the data is combined into an algorithm or spreadsheet, it requires an expert to interpret the results, the decision is a clinical one and the decision makers are applying their judgment.

❑   ❑   ❑

In this book we will make the case that investors will do substantially better if they use their judgment to create or select statistical methods rather than apply their judgment in the direct selection of individual securities.

The overwhelming majority of stockbrokers, portfolio managers, and individual investors select stocks using judgment, rather than SPMs. So when I say that you should use an algorithm, matrix, or set of rules to construct your portfolio, I am suggesting an approach radically different from what most people use.

Having an opinion that is diametrically opposed to almost everyone on Wall Street is a scary situation until you realize that if you invest the way everyone else does, you have no reason to expect better returns than everyone else gets.

To win at investing, you must have an approach that is different and better than the average investor's. I am not asking you to agree with me about this question; just keep an open mind. I will present empirical, logical, and anecdotal evidence that support my view that SPMs—or rules-based decision making—make the most sense for the majority of people. Then you can judge for yourself.

TRADITIONAL JUDGMENT METHOD
BUY OR AVOID

❏   ❏   ❏

Important Note!

I am advocating the use of statistical prediction methods when selecting a diversified, equally weighted, unleveraged equity portfolio as part of an overall financial plan. The strategies I advocate are completely transparent—I call them "naked"—relatively simple to implement, and can be explained on the back of a napkin.

STATISTICAL PREDICTION METHOD
BUY OR AVOID

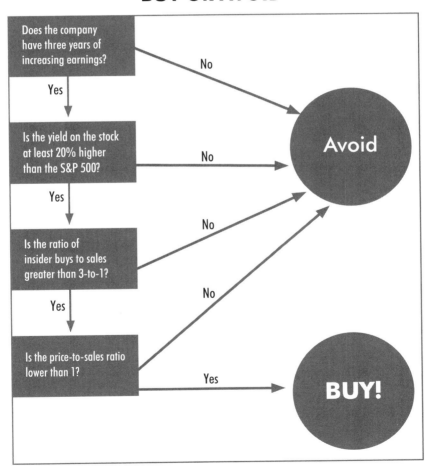

These strategies should not be confused with complex, esoteric, black box, leveraged strategies referred to as "quant" or quantitative strategies that are sometimes used by hedge funds and other very sophisticated investors.

Generally I think investors should avoid investments they do not understand, such as secret "black box" methodologies. As you will discover when reading this book, many very reliable SPMs require only a few pieces of relevant information to outperform the human judge.

❏   ❏   ❏

A Note on Stress and Investing

I have managed money through both clinical and statistical prediction methods. Judgment-based methods are extremely stressful and require you to interpret facts and make decisions that can be gut wrenching. The judgment-based system I used was called CAN SLIM, and it is the method recommended by Bill O'Neil, the founder of *Investor's Business Daily*. While the CAN SLIM method is an excellent approach, it is extremely difficult to implement and takes a huge emotional toll on the manager. This method requires interpretation of market direction and chart patterns that are often ambiguous. You have to cut losses quickly, and often you sell a stock and watch it go higher.

This method almost killed me. I had to come up with strategies that helped me deal with stress from all the difficult decisions I was making.

Naked portfolio management using SPMs is much easier on the central nervous system. Sure, sometimes I buy stocks that go down or sell stocks that go up, but I know this happens, and I continue to follow my system. This reduces the stress because I am not making difficult judgment calls.

I believe that over a lifetime of investing, statistical prediction methods will trounce judgment-based methods. An SPM should be considered successful if it beats the appropriate index six or seven years out of ten. Unfortunately, many people assume it is not working during the inevitable periods when it trails the market averages and give up on it. This type of thinking is wrongheaded. Short time periods of underperformance should be expected. Changing a winning strategy because of a short period of underperformance can lead to serious errors.

2

MASTERS OF DECISION MAKING— ARE THE BEST REALLY THE BEST?

Even highly trained decision makers, warriors of the mind, make inconsistent, emotional, and senseless decisions because they are human.

In order to understand why human judges are so consistently outperformed by statistical prediction models, let's look at the decision making of top chess grandmasters.

Classically trained decision-making machines, chess grandmasters are perhaps the best clinical decision makers on the planet. These masters rely heavily on prediction to determine how to play. In their thinking, they assume (predict) their opponent will always play the very best moves and thereby try to determine the correct course of action.

Grandmasters also combine a huge amount of data in their heads and make judgments about the best ways to proceed given the positions on the board.

One of the greatest chess players who ever lived was a fellow named Mikhail Tal, the youngest player ever to win the world chess championship and the only player to win four straight tournament games against chess legend Bobby Fischer. I was twelve years old when Bobby Fischer defeated Boris Spassky in

Reykjavik, Iceland, to win the world chess championship. The fact that we both are Robert J. Fischer and we both play chess is a coincidence.

In his autobiography, *The Life and Games of Mikhail Tal,* Tal describes a key game against Lajos Portisch, Hungary's best player in a tournament in 1965:

> [A]t a key point in the game I had to choose between transposing into a technically better position with a white knight on my queen four against a bishop on queen two and an isolated black pawn on his queen four, or playing for an attack. I chose the latter. After the game, Portisch asked me why I had not played differently at this point and played my rook to queen three. I replied that the move had not even entered my head. Portisch looked at me in astonishment, and said that I had already played the move in the exact same position in an earlier game. It was my turn to be astonished. "Where?" "When?" I asked. "At Curacao against Benko!"[3]

What surprised Tal was that he had solved the problem of what to play in an entirely different way for no apparent reason. It wasn't that he wanted to play differently against Portisch or that he had learned something new since the game with Benko. He simply forgot that he had played the position before.

We learn from this example that even the best clinical decision makers (chess grandmasters) are inconsistent in their decision making for reasons we can only guess.

There is another lesson we can learn from chess by studying the results of the 1997 match in which Deep Blue, an IBM supercomputer, took on Gary Kasparov, a player many consider to be history's second best player behind Bobby Fischer.

Kasparov had trounced the computer three wins to one with two draws the year earlier, and IBM was eager for a rematch. IBM had hired some of the world's top grandmasters to work with them to improve Deep Blue's play, and they felt they had a real chance to beat Kasparov. This match was to pit the world's best clinical decision maker, Kasparov, against what was probably the most advanced SPM ever developed.

The first game was uneventful, and Kasparov won without much difficulty as Deep Blue played in a fairly computer-like style.

In the second game, things were much different. Kasparov, playing the black pieces, drifted into a difficult position. He decided to sacrifice a couple of queen-side pawns to gain initiative. Kasparov thought while Deep Blue was busy shifting its pieces to the queen side to take the pawns, he could shift his pieces to the king side and begin a speculative attack against Deep Blue's king. Computers were notorious for going after pawns, and Kasparov expected that he could unbalance the game and perhaps grasp victory from the jaws of defeat.

Surprisingly, the computer played a very uncharacteristic defensive rook move and did not take the pawns. The position was too complicated for even Deep Blue to accurately calculate, so everyone expected the computer to grab the pawns since there was no clear refutation.

But it was as if the computer had said, "OK, I can win a couple of pawns, but my opponent is going to get a really strong attack, and who knows if I will be able to defend? I think the most prudent thing to do is improve my rook's position since my position is strong. I won't risk taking those pawns." Of course this is how people think. Computers think by comparing numbers, so Deep Blue's rook move was really startling.

After the mysterious rook move, Kasparov's position went downhill. Late in the game, Kasparov gave a final futile check in desperation, planning to resign after the computer moved. To get out of check, the computer could move its king to one of two squares. The computer moved and Kasparov resigned without checking the computer's move for accuracy as he would have done against a human player.

After the game, it was discovered that the computer had chosen an unsafe square for its king. It should have moved to the other square. It was a simple oversight pointed out by some of the players observing the match. Instead of resigning, Kasparov could have drawn the game.

The computer had played two very humanlike moves. One was a brilliant defensive move, and the other was a horrible blunder. Kasparov certainly would have exploited the blunder against a human, but he simply trusted the computer not to make that type of mistake. The score was one to one, but the match was over.

Kasparov's equanimity was wrecked. He suggested that IBM might be cheating—perhaps having a group of world-class players check Deep Blue's moves. He demanded to see the logs that explained how Deep Blue "thought," which IBM refused to provide, and threatened to quit the match.

After game two, Kasparov played more weakly. After a few draws, he lost the last game in only seventeen moves and with it, the match.

Most top grandmasters had expected Kasparov to win. When Kasparov accused the world's greatest SPM of cheating, the computer's feelings weren't hurt. It never threatened to quit the match, and it didn't retaliate with verbal assaults. Deep Blue never even demanded an apology. It just played.

The lesson here is that SPMs can outperform even the best clinical decision makers by being more consistent. Most grandmasters believed that Kasparov's judgment was superior to the machine's, so it was very surprising when Kasparov lost. But in the end, it did not matter as Kasparov was not able to bring that judgment to bear on the decisions he made.

This story illustrates one of the advantages naked portfolio managers have over traditional, judgment-based managers. Even if the portfolio manager normally makes better decisions than the SPM most of the time, life's occasional glitches can temporarily wreck his equanimity (maybe a close friend becomes seriously ill or his kid gets into trouble in school) and cause him to underperform in the long term against the naked manager.

I would like to add one more modern example from the world of chess that provides unique insight into how expert decision makers sometimes make irrational decisions. In October of 2007, the Tal memorial tournament was held in Moscow in honor of the late world champion. Ten of the world's best chess players were invited to play, including Alexey Shirov, ranked seventh in the world. Shirov annotated his game with Norwegian prodigy Magnus Carlsen in *New in Chess* magazine. With his nineteenth move, Carlsen took Shirov's rook with his bishop, and Shirov had to decide which piece he should use to capture the bishop. Shirov wrote:

> Here a rather strange incident occurred. I asked for a coffee. And in order to drink the coffee as quickly as possible, I captured [the bishop] with the rook, with hardly any thought. Later I somewhat regretted this. I should have analyzed which capture was stronger: with rook or queen …[4]

So here we have one of the top players in the world, playing in one of the most important tournaments of the year, admitting that he made his move without thinking so he could drink his coffee faster. This incident comically demonstrates that even world-class clinical decision makers sometimes make important decisions for totally inane reasons.

❏   ❏   ❏

If top grandmasters can make errors such as these, wouldn't you also expect top portfolio managers to occasionally make inconsistent, emotional, and senseless decisions?

3

Clinical versus Statistical Decision Making— The Studies

As human beings, we make a lot of decisions, but most of them are not really important.

When we are deciding what movie to watch or what we want for breakfast or how much to spend on a Christmas present, the decisions we make seldom have long-term consequences.

But sometimes we make decisions regarding our health, careers, children, or our money that have a profound influence on our futures. And how we make those decisions has proven to be fertile ground for psychologists trying to understand human behavior.

The first really important book on human decision making was *Clinical versus Statistical Prediction: A Theoretical Analysis and a Review of the Evidence,* published in 1954 by psychologist Paul Meehl, a leading philosopher and an independent thinker. Meehl later became known for developing new approaches to hypothesis testing and for his contribution to the Minnesota Multiphasic Personality Inventory, a psychometric test that enables clinicians to understand certain aspects of human psychology. But he is most famous for what he came to call his "disturbing little book."[5]

In his book, Meehl made the case for using SPMs instead of clinical decision making. He theorized that human judges would make more mistakes than a mechanical prediction tool created for a similar decision-making purpose. Mechanical prediction methods, he explained, are simply ways of combining data to arrive at a decision or prediction.

Meehl was not saying that human judgment was not useful for making predictions. His point was that clinicians are often inconsistent when applying human judgment in their predictions. That is to say, they sometimes make one decision one time and, given the exact same fact set, make a different decision the next time.

SPMs never do this. The mechanical decision-making tool will make the exact same prediction for the exact same data every time.

Meehl's theory shook the field of psychology to its core. At the time, the prevailing opinion was that clinicians had special powers or predictive abilities that could never be captured in a statistical model. He was in essence telling practicing psychologists that they were wrong about human decision making.

Many clinicians wrote caustic articles criticizing Meehl's contention; he quotes from some of these in his book:

> "...standardization by its very nature [by using models] ignores the individual" and "The statistical point of view must be supplemented by the clinical point of view" and "Such a schematization would be incompatible with basic principles..."[6]

Twelve years after Meehl's book was published, Jack Sawyer published a meta-analysis of forty-five studies comparing clinical and statistical methods of decision making. In Sawyer's studies the clinicians sometimes had more data than was used to construct the statistical models. It didn't matter. In no case were the clinicians better able to predict than the SPMs.[7] Many other studies have been done since Sawyer's book was published.

In 1954 Meehl was just a young (thirty-four-year-old) professor with an unproven iconoclastic theory that certainly didn't make him many friends. But through the years, scientists conducted many tests of Meehl's theory, and time and again, studies showed that SPM-based decisions produced better results than clinically based decisions. In fact, in a 2005 article in the *Journal of Clinical Psychology*, Robyn Dawes cites 135 studies comparing SPMs to clinical decision making. SPMs did as well or better than the clinicians in all but a handful of studies. The few in which human judges performed better could be explained by chance or, more likely, a situation in which the judges had more information than did the SPM. Many of these studies were summarized in his book *House of Cards: Psychology and Psychotherapy Built on Myth.*[8]

One of the studies was of a University of Texas Medical School class. The study showed that the decision making of the admissions committee (human decision makers applying their judgment) was no better than even very simple SPMs.

Here is what happened. For the class entering in 1979, the school had 2,200 applications for 150 available openings. The admissions department interviewed 800 applicants and ranked them from 1 to 800 based on the judgments from the admissions committee. The school filled its 150 openings with the students ranked by the admissions officers (judges) in the top 350 based on their interviews.

However, in April of 1979, the Texas legislature required the school to increase its number of students in the class to 200. The school had a problem; the only applicants left were the ones who had the worst rankings on the admission officers' ratings.

These students had been passed over by the University of Texas Medical School and most other medical schools, while most of the higher-ranked applicants had already accepted invitations to attend other schools.

So the University of Texas had to round out its class with 50 students who had been rejected by most of the medical schools where they applied and, based on the judgment of the admissions committee, were the worst applicants with the least chance of success in medical school.

So how did these 50 students do in medical school? Just fine. In fact, in an article published in the *Journal of the American Medical Association* titled "Medical School Performance of Initially

Rejected Students," R. A. DeVaul and others concluded there was no difference in performance between the initially rejected students and those selected first. Their graduation rates, spread of grade point averages, and percentages of honor students were all the same as the higher-ranked group.

The article makes the point that the admissions committee spent an enormous amount of time and money interviewing the applicants, writing reports, and analyzing the results of these interviews when a simple statistical model could have predicted the likelihood of success just as well (maybe better depending on how it was constructed). It would also have saved the 800 students interviewed and the admissions committee countless hours and thousands of dollars.[9]

Other studies that Dawes reviewed include a study that analyzed how the Pennsylvania Parole Board judged 1,095 inmates who had parole hearings between October 1977 and May 1978. The parole board's judgments were compared to SPMs based on the type of offense, the number of prior convictions, the number of prison rule violations, and past heroin use. Again, the SPMs predicted the rate of recidivism and the likelihood of violence more accurately than the parole board did.

More recently, in 2001, two political scientists, Andrew Martin and Kevin Quinn, claimed they had developed an SPM that could predict, based on a limited amount of data, how the Supreme Court would decide appeals cases.

Ted Ruger, a law professor at the University of Pennsylvania, thought this was hogwash, so he challenged the political scientists to compare the predictions of the model to the collective judgments of a team of legal luminaries. The team included thirty-eight attorneys who had clerked for a Supreme Court justice, thirty-three attorneys who held chaired professorships, and five law school deans.

The SPM used only six variables:

1. The circuit court of origin
2. The issue area of the case

3. The type of petitioner
4. The type of respondent
5. The ideological direction (liberal or conservative) of the lower court
6. Whether or not the petitioner argued that a law or practice was unconstitutional

Both the political scientists and the lawyers posted their predictions on a Web site prior to the Supreme Court's 2002 rulings.

The attorneys lost. They were right in predicting the court's ruling 59 percent of the time, while the SPM, based on only six clearly defined and easily identifiable variables, was right 75 percent of the time.[10]

Of course, this book is not titled *The Naked Attorney* because it is about the stock market. But the fact that a statistical model that considered only six variables was able to crush the collective judgments of a group of the best legal minds who knew those variables and much more has profound implications for investors. In this case, more information certainly did not lead to better predictions.

❑   ❑   ❑

Another recent example of the power of SPMs was described in the best-selling book *Blink: The Power of Thinking without Thinking* by Malcolm Gladwell in which an SPM took on a group of physicians in 1996 and 1997. In the book, Gladwell relates the story of Brendan Reilly, a Dartmouth-educated hospital administrator who put Meehl's theory to the test in the hospital emergency room.

Reilly came to Cook County Hospital in Chicago during an extremely difficult time. As Gladwell relates in his book:

> The institution Reilly had inherited was a mess. As the city's principal public hospital, Cook County was the place of last resort for hundreds of thousands of Chicagoans without health insurance. Resources were stretched to the limit.

Many of the people who used this hospital were poor and had no health insurance. At the time, the hospital faced many challenges, but the most pressing problem was the lack of beds available to treat patients suffering from chest pains. Every day the hospital's emergency ward was seeing about thirty patients complaining of chest pains and worried they were having a heart attack. Reilly didn't have the beds in his cardiac unit or the money in his budget to treat them all as heart attack patients.

Reilly knew there were ways to tell with absolute certainty whether someone was having a heart attack, but these involved testing for particular enzymes and could take hours. Of course, when a person came into the emergency room complaining of chest pains, there was no time for such tests.

The hospital's doctors needed to make a decision immediately. They had three choices: (1) treat the patient as a heart attack victim and admit him to the cardiac unit for intensive and expensive treatment, (2) admit him to the hospital for observation and further testing, or (3) simply prescribe aspirin and bed rest and send him home.

Many doctors, however, were erring on the side of caution by admitting patients to the cardiac ward for observation even if, after an initial examination, they did not appear to be having heart attacks.

Given his scarce resources, Reilly did not have the luxury to continue this practice. It was imperative he separate the patients truly having heart attacks from those with merely acute cases of heartburn.[11]

As a solution, he turned to a decision tree developed for the U.S. Navy by cardiologist Lee Goldman. The Navy was interested in a decision matrix for use in submarines. If a sub were spying in enemy waters and a sailor started to complain of chest pains, the submariners needed to know if it were absolutely necessary to surface and medevac the sailor—thus giving away the sub's position—or if they could just send him to sick bay with some antacids.

Goldman compiled and tested data from thousands of patients to develop a method for determining an appropriate level of care for a patient suffering from chest pains. He worked on his algorithm for years to create a simple decision tree based on just four variables: the electrocardiogram reading, blood pressure, fluid in the lungs, and angina.

Reilly knew he would have to do a lot of work with his staff before they would trust the chest pain decision tree. As he explained to me in an e-mail:

> [W]e did a lot of work with the ED [Emergency Department] docs and other docs (who take over after the ED doc's initial decision) before we implemented the decision rule in actual practice. If we had not done this preparatory work, the project would never have happened...the docs had to learn to trust the rule.

He further explained that even after educating the doctors about how rigorously Goldman's team had developed and validated the rule, the doctors insisted on some changes before they would use it on real patients.

Reilly acknowledged the model outperformed the clinical, judgment-based decisions of the doctors because it reduced the occurrence of unnecessary hospitalizations. The model "outperformed" the doctors in the sense that it reduced the use of unnecessary resources, that is, it avoided hospitalizing patients who didn't need the hospital (termed "efficiency"). It did not outperform the doctors (but it was just as good) in deciding which patients did need the hospital (termed "safety").

He pointed out a key issue, though: both the model and the doctors were concerned with the safety of the patients and about the efficient use of resources, but the doctors cared much more about safety than they cared about efficiency. They understandably had a built-in bias toward protecting the patient.

But as Reilly wrote to me, "when these two complementary metrics [efficiency and safety] are considered together, the rule did better than the docs."

❏   ❏   ❏

So what does all this have to do with managing a stock portfolio? Plenty. Portfolio managers are very much like Reilly's physicians when making decisions.

The emergency room doctors were making their decisions using various objective factors such as age, weight, sex, and medical history, combined with subjective factors, which may or may not be honestly reported by the patient (such as how much exercise he gets and how frequently he eats fatty foods).

Portfolio managers, in turn, try to determine the likelihood that a stock will appreciate by studying objective factors such as price-to-earnings ratios, revenue, and profit margins, combined with subjective factors such as the chief executive officer's vision of the future of the company (similarly, not always honestly reported).

Constructing a winning naked portfolio management system is very much like the work Goldman did in constructing his heart attack decision tree. A large amount of data must be sifted through and tested to find the right variables. But once that has been done, application of the rules is relatively simple.

If a set of carefully researched rules, applied uniformly and dispassionately in the emergency room, can dramatically improve human decisions, saving lives and money, why couldn't a similar set of rules dramatically improve the decision making of an investor and meaningfully improve his long-term investment returns?

Common Thinking Errors

Introduction:
Thinking Errors

O f all God's creations, nothing is more wonderful than the human mind. Human thinking has given us Shakespeare's plays, Beethoven's music, and the Golden Gate Bridge, and it has even put a man on the moon. Human thinking is able to discern the most subtle things, such as when a smile means happiness and when it means sadness or how the same words can express caring or sarcasm depending on the tone in which they are spoken. So with all the great things the human mind can do, you would think making good decisions would be pretty simple. The evidence would indicate that it is not.

We have contrasted SPMs to clinical decision makers in the emergency room of Cook County Hospital and learned that SPMs save lives and money over the decisions of expert clinical cardiologists. We have analyzed the results of clinical decision making by the University of Texas Medical School and learned that thousands of man-hours and a vast amount of money were wasted trying to identify the best candidates for medical school when a simple SPM could have done the same job at least as well for a fraction of the cost. We have seen how the best legal minds were whipped by a simple matrix that could be drawn on a napkin. We have examined the thinking of some of the best intuitive thinkers of all time, top chess grandmasters, and found their thought processes inconsistent. Perhaps now is the time to discuss why human judges have such a tough time making optimal decisions.

A review of the literature suggests that humans make three broad categories of mistakes when applying their judgment:

1. People fail to properly use information they already have, a mistake we call fuzzy thinking.
2. People don't understand sophisticated concepts.
3. People fail to understand that some problems are beyond the ability of the human mind to solve.

Accordingly, the following chapters will focus on simple decision-making errors, complex thinking errors, intractable thinking errors, and a special case—confirmation bias.

4

SIMPLE DECISION-MAKING ERRORS, AKA FUZZY THINKING

My favorite episode of *Star Trek* illustrates one type of simple decision-making error—**fuzzy thinking.** In this episode, Spock, Bones, Scotty, and several other members of the crew are in a small craft that crashes on an uncharted planet.

While Scotty works feverishly to fix the craft so they can return to the starship *Enterprise,* a few other members of the crew go out to reconnoiter the area. Unfortunately, the inhabitants of the planet are hostile, and they kill some of the crew members. Understandably, the crew is very angry, and some of the men want to take their phasers and get even with the creatures that attacked their crewmates. The ever-logical and unemotional Spock reminds the crew that all life is valuable and that killing some of the planet's inhabitants will not bring back their dead comrades. Instead, Spock and the crew go out and use their phasers to blow up some rocks and trees to demonstrate their superior firepower.

Spock reckons this demonstration of force will keep the hostile inhabitants away and give the crew time to repair the craft. Much to Spock's surprise, the creatures attack the ship. Spock cannot understand why they are acting so illogically since he and his crew had clearly demonstrated their superior firepower.

Both Spock and the crew are guilty of fuzzy thinking. While the crew's emotional desire to counterattack is understandable, it is also wrong. First, by leading an expedition to attack the large, furry creatures, they would unnecessarily put themselves in harm's way. Next, if they found large, furry creatures, how would they know if those were the creatures that killed their crewmates? Last, an attack would expend their phasers' energy, and as it turned out, the energy in the phasers was necessary to launch their craft back into space.

Spock's mistake is also a classic case of fuzzy thinking in that he assumes the creatures think as he does. Had Spock considered the situation, he probably would have said to himself, "These large, furry creatures attacked my shipmates unprovoked and killed them for no reason. Why should I assume they think like a Vulcan?" He might have made a better decision had he thought the problem through more thoroughly.

Although this example is from science fiction, it clearly demonstrates fuzzy thinking.

In the past twenty years, a new field of psychology called behavioral finance has made considerable advances in understanding how and why we make poor decisions. Two PhDs, Amos Tversky and Daniel Kahneman, pioneered work in understanding why humans make certain types of errors regarding their investment decisions.

As investors, it is important to understand thinking errors and decision-making mistakes for a couple of reasons. First, we want to avoid making these mistakes ourselves, and more important, we want to select investment strategies that are designed to take advantage of the systematic thinking errors of others.

With this in mind, below is a short list of some of the typical errors identified by Kahneman and Tversky. All of these errors fall into the same type of error that Spock made—fuzzy thinking. People should know better, but often they don't.

OVERCONFIDENCE

Human beings are consistently overconfident. In their book *Judgment under Uncertainty: Heuristics and Biases,* Kahneman and Tversky cite numerous studies that show that human beings have far more belief in their predictive abilities than is justified. They found this to be true whether the subjects of their experiments were college students or PhDs.

For example, in a case study in their book, a group of psychologists and psychology students were given data about a patient named Joseph Kidd and asked to make diagnostic predications about his future behavior. The group consisted of eight clinical psychologists employed by a California state hospital with several years of clinical experience, eighteen psychology graduate students, and six advanced undergraduate students in a class on personality.

The subjects were given four sets of data, one at a time. In the first set, they learned basic demographic information about Kidd, including his age, occupation, marital status, and the fact that he was a veteran of the armed services.

With the next three sets of data, each presenting new information, they learned about his childhood to age twelve, his high school and college experiences, and his military and life experiences as an adult.

The test group was asked a series of multiple-choice personality questions after they received each set of data. Then they were asked to estimate, as a group, their percentage of correct answers.

Each time they received a new set of data, they were offered the opportunity to change their previous answers and again asked to estimate their percentage of correct answers.

With each new set of data they received, the subjects gained more confidence in their predications. For example, after stage one the group estimated they had answered correctly 33 percent of the time. And by the time they had all four sets of data, the group reported 53 percent confidence in their predictions.

However, the group's accuracy in their predictions did not increase. Their percentage of correct answers after receiving one set of data was about the same as after receiving all four sets. More information did not lead to better decision making. Also, despite their experience, the psychologists alone did not predict more successfully than the students did.[12]

Kahneman and Tversky did a number of other tests in which they asked a variety of subjects to make predictions. In almost all of the tests, the subjects grossly overestimated their abilities to make accurate predictions. In fact, the tendency of human beings to overestimate their abilities in a variety of decision-making scenarios is one of the most documented social tendencies.

As an investment professional, I frequently see overconfidence causing investors to make poor decisions. For example, I occasionally get calls telling me to sell everything because the market is going down. I will ask the client why he is so confident the market will be lower. Usually I will get an ill-considered justification based on some generality that he heard on television.

Believing you can predict the direction of the market based on what you hear on television or read in the newspaper is a classic example of overconfidence. When pressed, these clients will usually admit they have no special talent or knowledge that allows them to divine the direction of the market. Nevertheless, they sell their stocks, despite the fact that they realize it is a poor decision.

Commitment Bias

This refers to following through on a decision, despite compelling evidence that it is wrong. This could also be called dogmatic thinking or simply being stubborn. A study of gamblers conducted by a pair of Canadian psychologists suggested that when people commit money to a decision, their confidence rises. The psychologists explained this behavior as a basic human desire to be consistent with what we have already done. Once we have taken a position, we will encounter personal and interpersonal pressures to behave in a way that is consistent with the position we have taken.

Commitment bias can cause people to make horrific mistakes in the stock market. One investor told me a story of how he had a $500,000 profit on Nortel stock. He did not want to sell it and pay taxes. He became so committed to his decision to avoid the taxes that he watched in horror as his $500,000 profit turned into a loss.

Group Think

This is all about conforming to the group. Do you remember the old *Candid Camera* television show with Alan Funt? In this television show, similar to Ashton Kutcher's recent series called *Punk'd,* people were secretly filmed while actors played a joke on them by behaving in a very unusual or inappropriate way. The show succeeded because the reactions of the subjects were so humorous to watch.

There was one very funny episode involving an elevator. When a subject got on the elevator, everyone else on the elevator would turn and face the rear wall. Their "victim" would look very uncomfortable at first then would usually turn slowly and face the back of the elevator to conform to everyone else. Then, on cue, the people in the elevator would turn ninety degrees and face the side of the elevator. Gradually the person would turn to conform to the group.

It was very funny to watch, but it has a very important learning point about the very natural human desire to conform to the group. When you think about this tendency, it helps to understand why Wall Street so frequently overpays for certain types of stocks, whether they be tech stocks in the nineties, oil stocks in the eighties, or growth stocks in the sixties.

Anchoring

This is the tendency for people to fixate on numbers and use them when making estimations or predictions, even in circumstances when it does not make sense to do so.

For example, Kahneman and Tversky did an amusing experiment in which they asked subjects to spin a roulette wheel. After a random number came up, they asked the subjects to look at the number on the wheel guess the number of African countries that belonged to the United Nations.

Curiously, even though the subjects knew the number on the wheel was random and had nothing at all to do with the question, they tended to anchor on it. Those whose numbers were low, estimated a low number of African nations. Those with a high number on the wheel guessed a high number.[13]

In his book *The Black Swan: The Impact of the Highly Improbable*, Nassim Nicholas Taleb gives another example of people anchoring on irrelevant numbers. He reports on an experiment where he asked people to list the last four digits of their Social Security numbers. He then asked them to estimate the number of dentists in Manhattan. Despite the fact that these two numbers cannot possibly be related in any way, he found the people's estimates of the number of dentists to be correlated with the last four digits of their Social Security numbers.[14]

People's tendency to anchor on prices, combined with their need to be correct, is sometimes more important to them than the desire to make money. This causes them to be unwilling to purchase a stock selling for more than when they first started watching it.

Warren Buffet, lamenting the fact he had not bought more Wal-Mart stock, said, "We've missed billions when I've gotten anchored ... I set out to buy 100 million shares, pre-split, at $23. We bought a little and it moved up and I thought it might come back a little bit ... the reluctance to pay a little more cost us a lot." If a man as brilliant as Warren Buffet can get anchored, it is easy to see why it happens so frequently to ordinary investors.

People can anchor on a stock's price, dividend yield, price-to-earnings ratio, or any of a variety of other numbers. For example, during the seventies, eighties, and early nineties, one of the rules of thumb was to sell stocks any time the yield on the S&P 500 dipped below 3 percent, and many people anchored on this number.

In late 1995, when the market's yield dipped to 2.3 percent and its price-to-earnings ratios approached 20, many investors, anchored to these numbers, sold stocks, believing that stock prices were a bubble about to burst.

But as David Shulman of Salomon Brothers explained in a December 1995 piece titled "1996: Stock Market Bubble or Paradigm Shift,"

> [W]e are beginning to allow for the possibility that the valuation clocks we have been using are broken; the powerful 1995 rally in stock prices is not a bubble, but rather a signal that the valuation paradigm has changed.[15]

He was right of course. In 1996 the S&P 500 appreciated 23 percent. That was followed by a return of 33.4 percent in 1997, 28.6 percent in 1998, and 21 percent in 1999. Investors anchored to their 3 percent dividend rule sat on the sidelines and missed one of the greatest bull markets ever.

Emotional Connections

These can cause professionals to make mistakes they otherwise wouldn't make. In his excellent book *How Doctors Think,* Jerome Groopman, MD, gives several examples of how doctors' feelings about patients cause them to make errors in determining the best treatments.

In one particularly poignant example, Groopman tells of a cancer patient named Brad Miller, who was a medical doctor and a marathon runner. Groopman, who used to be a runner himself, developed a great rapport with Brad. One day, Groopman, while checking Brad's eyes, nose, throat, and abdomen, decided that Brad, exhausted from three treatments of chemotherapy and in obvious pain, had had enough prodding for one day and truncated his examination. The standard procedure, which Groopman failed to complete, required Brad to roll on his stomach to continue the examination. Groopman short-circuited the procedure out of an emotional desire to reduce Brad's discomfort.

Unfortunately, Brad had developed abscesses on his buttocks and suffered septic shock later that day. This, of course, could have been avoided had Groopman followed the established procedure. His failure to do so was the result of his emotional connection with his patient. It was more important to do a thorough examination than to avoid causing further discomfort for the patient.

The point of the story is that a clinician or human decision maker, because he truly likes and cares for his patients, can sometimes make decisions that cause problems for them, whereas following established protocols would have avoided these difficulties.[16]

This example has profound implications for the stock market investor. Analysts and portfolio managers following companies for long periods of time frequently develop relationships with management. If an analyst or portfolio manager has an excellent, long-lasting relationship with a CEO, is it possible this affects his willingness to ask particularly difficult questions? *Could the fact that Ken Lay and Jeff Skilling were especially kind to Wall Street analysts have anything to do with the fact that so few analysts asked the really tough questions of top Enron management?*

AVAILABILITY

This is another factor that affects human decisions. If you ask someone to name three deceased United States presidents, who would they name? My guess is that they would say George Washington, Abraham Lincoln, and Ronald Reagan. I think this answer is much more likely than the chance they would say Martin Van Buren, Millard Fillmore, and James Buchanan, although this answer is equally correct.

If I asked you to name all the presidents whose first names began with a G, you would probably say George Washington, both George Herbert Walker Bush and George W. Bush, and Gerald Ford. But you might miss Grover Cleveland. If I asked you to name all the presidents whose last names began with a vowel, I think you would remember Dwight Eisenhower and John Adams, but would you remember John Quincy Adams and Chester Arthur?

Certain facts are more available to our subconscious and easier to recall. Availability causes distortion when human judges try to recall facts that influence their decisions. Since some facts are easier to recall, decision makers frequently use these facts and fail to assign appropriate weight to facts that are difficult to recall.

For example, stocks from well-known companies may become more attractive to an investor for no other reason than that they are household names.

Influence of Recent Events

This is an availability situation that can also have profound effects on the way people make decisions. After the release of the movie *Jaws,* about a huge shark that terrorizes a small coastal community, many people stayed away from the beaches in droves. This occurred despite the fact that shark attacks on humans are extremely rare and statisticians will argue that you are more likely to be injured driving to the beach in an automobile accident than to be attacked by a great white shark.

Stories

So what lessons can we draw from *Jaws* for the traditional portfolio manager and the naked portfolio manager?

Simply this: the traditional manager can be susceptible to very powerful stories, another subset of the availability problem.

People who make decisions using their judgment can sometimes let their reasoning become distorted by a compelling narrative. Extremely vivid and powerful stories about great companies, new industries, and other opportunities that capture the imagination are common on Wall Street.

These stories are more plentiful than dull but equally important data that suggest the great stock or new industry may *not* have unlimited potential.

To see this, take a trip to your local library and look at the covers of financial and business publications. In March of 2000, just before the Internet bubble burst, *Smart Money* magazine's cover read, *15 great tech stocks.* The featured article urgently crowed about the sectors that investors must own to profit from the coming opportunities in technology investing.

The reader was urged to take advantage of opportunities in fifteen technology stocks in order to maximize gains. These stocks, described by the magazine article as the "Ultimate Tech Portfolio," were expected to "light a fire under your overall holdings."[17]

So what were the ultimate stocks that would light such a fire? Would you have gotten rich following the advice of *Smart Money*? Take a look at the stocks:

PMC-Sierrra (PMCS)

JDS Uniphase (JDSU)

Cisco Systems (CSCO)

Applied Materials (AMAT)

RF Micro Devices (AMAT)

Taiwan Semiconductor Mfg. (TSM)

Arriba (ARBA)

LSI Logic (LSI)

Lucent (LU)

ADC Telecommunications (ADCT)

Powerwave Technologies (PWAV)

Sanmina Corp (SANM)

Hyperion Solutions (HYSL)

Parametric Technology (PMTC)

At the time of this writing, eight years after the *Smart Money* article, none of the stocks is showing a profit. Of those still trading under the same symbol, all are down more than 50 percent. JDS Uniphase and Arriba are down more than 98 percent. Even Cisco is down 75 percent. For more information, you can go to www.bigcharts.com and track the progress of these stocks.

Of course, it was not just *Smart Money* readers who got sandbagged with these stocks. If you review the holdings of popular mutual funds, you will find that many of these disaster stocks found their way into the top holdings. And if, while you are at the library, you stop and pull a copy of the February 2001 mutual fund ratings of any of the popular financial tabloids, you will see a full-blown horror show with many funds down more than 50 percent from a year earlier.

Why were they down so much? The fund managers had bought into the story, literally and figuratively. It was a simple, compelling story that said a new technology is going to revolutionize the way we do business in this world. You had better get a piece of it because these stocks are going to the moon and you don't want to miss it.

History is clear; investing in new technology is not an easy way to stock market riches.

Extremely powerful stories can cause people, including portfolio managers, to make poor decisions. The only surefire defense against this type of thinking error is to stick rigidly to naked portfolio management strategies.

Naked portfolio managers never get caught up in stories, no matter how exciting.

❏　　❏　　❏

I know that many people and portfolio managers will protest that their thinking is structured, disciplined, and systematic and that stories play no part in their decision making. I think they are deceiving themselves.

I would like to offer a recent experience of mine that will show how insidious thinking errors can be. This story occurred when I was writing this book, so I was constantly asking myself what thinking errors I needed to watch out for in all my decisions.

On a recent Easter vacation, I took my children and nephew to Orlando to the Universal Studios theme park. On the first day we parked in the Jaws parking lot. On the second day, we parked in the Spider-Man lot. On the third day, we parked in … well, that's where the story gets interesting.

On the third day we parked on the top level, and I noted our row number, 516, and mentioned it to my son, Robby, who was eleven years old. After several hours of riding rides, we headed back to our car. I said to my son, "We are in Spider-Man 516, right?" He responded in the affirmative. Then my ten-year-old nephew, Christopher, piped in and said that we were in the Jaws parking lot.

Robby and I told him that he was confused and that we had parked in Jaws on the first day. He was adamant as we walked toward the Spider-Man parking garage, insisting that when we came to the park that day, we had walked by a SpongeBob SquarePants exhibit and, since we did not see SpongeBob, we must be going the wrong way.

Neither my son nor I listened to him. When we got to the Spider-Man garage, there was no row 516. In fact, the fifth level was not the top floor of the lot. We searched for our car for twenty minutes, going to the sixth level and thinking maybe we had transposed the digits of the row. We didn't want to walk to the Jaws lot, which was at the other end of the parking area, several hundred yards away (commitment bias). My ten-year-old nephew kept insisting that since we had not passed SpongeBob, we were in the wrong lot.

Finally, just to rule out the possibility that he was right, my son and I decided to go to the Jaws lot. We walked to the other parking garage, past the SpongeBob exhibit, to the Jaws lot, to row 516, and to our car.

Here is the interesting thing about this story. The last ride we took that day was a three-dimensional ride named Spider-Man. On this ride, Spider-Man swung from buildings, hopped on the front of our scoop, and fought diabolical villains. Spider-Man was definitely on our minds as we left the theme park (availability error).

There is a lesson in this for all decision makers. First, recent vivid images can affect a person's thinking. But there is a more subtle lesson. I grew up with Spider-Man cartoons and comic books. I like Spider-Man. I did not grow up with SpongeBob as he had not been created when I was a boy. When my nephew protested that we had not passed the SpongeBob exhibit, I discounted it because I am much less familiar with SpongeBob. I was wrong, of course, to discount this, but this is a typical error that a clinical decision maker makes—discounting certain information because he does not like it or is not comfortable with the nature or the source of the information.

Here is the amazing thing. I have studied how availability, commitment, and subtle prejudices (liking Spider-Man more than SpongeBob) can affect a person's thinking. But knowing about these tendencies was not enough to keep me from making these types of errors.

❑   ❑   ❑

I believe that clinical decision makers, especially portfolio managers, make the types of errors I made in the parking lot all the time. They like one company because it has a pristine balance sheet and dislike another because the balance sheet has some holes, and they discount the fact that the company with the imperfect balance sheet is growing at a much faster rate.

They do this because they were praised by their bosses in an earlier job for recommending companies with excellent balance sheets, and it makes them feel comfortable to recommend companies with similar balance sheets. Or a portfolio manager might like the management of one company because the CEO is a tall, blond man who reminds him of his father and dislike another company because the CEO is a short, fat woman who reminds him of his third-grade teacher. He probably doesn't realize he has these biases and prejudices, but they are there. And the only dependable way to avoid these types of errors is to use statistical prediction methods.

Kahneman and Tversky found many other biases and heuristics (rules of thumb used to make decisions) that prevent people from making optimal decisions. All of these examples are cases that might have been avoided by using logic in an unemotional, calculating way and asking oneself dispassionately if this is the optimal approach to decision making. The next set of thinking errors we will discuss is more complicated and cannot be avoided by rational analysis.

┌─────┐
│ 5 │
└─────┘

COMPLEX THINKING ERRORS

W hat do the examples from the last chapter with Warren Buffet, Dr. Jerome Groopman, and Spock have in common? All three were quick to realize when they were guilty of fuzzy thinking.

And while fuzzy thinking is easy to identify with hindsight, this is not so with this next group of errors. Investors can make this type of error time and again without realizing it. People need formal training to avoid this type of error.

❏   ❏   ❏

In his book *The Limits of Scientific Reasoning,* David Faust identifies the failure to understand sophisticated concepts as an example of a complex decision-making error.

For example, Faust cites a study done in 1974 by Kahneman and Tversky that shows that people frequently will make **extreme predictions based on insufficient data.** In the study, individuals were asked the likelihood a person would succeed based on a single piece of information. The test group was given a short paragraph describing how well a student teacher performed on a lesson and asked how likely the student would be successful as a teacher five years hence.

When the paragraph described the lesson as excellently prepared, the test subjects predicted he or she would be very successful as a teacher. If the student's lesson were poorly prepared, the test subjects predicted the teacher would be a failure. The key point of the study was that there was not enough information to predict success or failure, so predictions should have concentrated about the mean, that is, regardless of how the lesson went, the student was about as likely as average to succeed.

But the test subjects did not do this. They made extreme predictions about a person's career potential based on a tiny amount of information. This type of error is not fuzzy thinking or poor thinking habits. It results from a failure to understand a sophisticated statistical concept: when making estimations, you should predict near the mean unless there is a compelling reason to make an extreme prediction.

Suggesting the teacher would be a failure is an extreme prediction. One poorly prepared lesson is not a justification for making this type of prediction. This is like concluding that a high school student will never graduate from college based on one bad quiz grade. It is illogical to make extreme predictions based on limited information.

Making estimates close to the mean or average is the most reliable prediction method with limited information, and extreme predictions should be made only when there is compelling evidence to reject the mean.

So how does this principle apply to portfolio management? When judgment-based portfolio managers make extreme predictions far into the future, they are guilty of this error, and the results can be disastrous.

Consider that the 1970 forecast by U.S. officials (signed by the U.S. Secretaries of the Treasury, State, the Interior, and Defense) stated, "The standard price of foreign crude oil by 1980 may well decline and in any case will not experience a substantial increase." Yet by 1980 oil prices had increased tenfold.[18]

So imagine how a portfolio manager in 1970, relying on this inaccurate forecast, might make errors in his portfolio construction by assuming that energy prices would rise modestly or even decline.

Fortunately, the naked portfolio manager does not rely on economic forecasts.

Ignoring the base rate (or prior odds) is another thinking error that results from a failure to understand sophisticated statistical concepts. Consider another Kahneman and Tversky study that Faust discusses in his book. Subjects were given a piece of information about an individual then asked to guess his profession. Here is an example:

> Dick is a thirty-year-old man. He is married with no children. A man of high ability and high motivation, he promises to be quite successful in his field. He is well liked by his colleagues.[19]

With one hundred descriptions that were similarly ambiguous, the test group was asked to guess whether the person described was an accountant or an attorney. Sometimes the group was told there were seventy lawyers and thirty accountants; other times they were told seventy accountants and thirty lawyers.

The base rate (or odds) for each described person to be a lawyer or accountant was 70 percent, depending on what the group was told.

But even though the descriptions were so ambiguous as to be useless for predicting occupations, the test subjects consistently ignored the base rate and used the descriptive information to make a decision.

In my own practice, I have frequently seen investors ignore base rates, which frequently costs them money. When investors place long-term money, such as IRA money they will not use for twenty or more years, in money markets or certificates of deposit, they are ignoring base rates.

What I will point out to them is that the long-term average of stocks (the base rate) is about 9 percent per year and is much higher than the rate on the money market fund. Unless they have some extraordinary ability to predict when the market is going up or down, putting their long-term money into money funds (e.g., at 3 percent per year) instead of stocks will cost on average about ½ percent per month in expected return.

Since we expect over the long run that stocks will beat cash, when an investor puts long-term money into cash, he is making the same bet as the individual who said in the Kahneman and Tversky study referenced above, Dick was an accountant when told that 70 percent of the people described in the group were lawyers.

Ignoring the base rate is never a problem for the naked portfolio manager since, by definition, naked portfolio management is base-rate investing.

It is here we see the greatest contrast between naked portfolio management and traditional judgment-based methods. Judgment-based managers frequently believe their superior insight or "special powers" give them the ability to identify trends or securities that uninspired, statistical number crunching misses. As we shall see when we review the record of judgment-based managers, they are wrong more often than they are right.

Faust identifies another complex decision-making error—the **failure to understand the law of small numbers.** He gives an example where Stanford University undergraduates (a group of very smart people) were told that two hospitals were doing a study of the number of boys born each day. In hospital A about forty-five babies were born each day, and in hospital B about fifteen babies were born daily. The students were asked which hospital was more likely to have 60 percent or more newborn boys on a given day.

The fundamental principle involved here is that large samples are much less likely to deviate from the mean than small samples; the students should have said that hospital B was more likely to have 60 percent boys than hospital A. However, more than half of the students answered that each hospital was equally likely to have 60 percent boys on a given day. The remaining answers were equally split between the two hospitals, so less than 25 percent of the students got the question right.

Kahneman and Tversky concluded from this study that "the notion that sampling variance decreases in proportion to sample size is apparently not part of man's repertoire of intuitions."[20] Said another way, most people incorrectly believe that if you take a small sample from a group, the sample will behave the same way as a much larger sample taken from the same group.

Again, in my practice I have seen investors misapply the law of small numbers. A corollary to the law of small numbers is a rule that I call the rule of short time periods.

Investors make the same mistake when they expect a strategy that performs well over the long term to perform equally well over the short term. You can see this when a mutual fund has underperformed for a period of time. The investor concludes that something is wrong and wants to change the investment. I have had clients tell me they want to leave a particular fund that has trailed the market for six months or three months or even shorter periods. A misunderstanding of the rule of short time periods causes this.

To illustrate this point, let's say you invest in a mutual fund because you believe the manager to be extraordinarily gifted. Let's say that you are right and the portfolio manager can be expected to beat his index on an annual basis 60 percent of the time. Let's also assume that when he beats his benchmark, he beats it by, on average, 3 percent, and when he trails the benchmark, he trails it by 3 percent. That would be a record most portfolio managers would be delighted to produce. If you hired such a manager, what is the probability that over the next fifteen years, there would be a period in which the manager trailed the market for three consecutive years? What are the chances the manager would trail for four consecutive years? Remember, this is a manager we expect to beat the market 60 percent of the time.

Most investors are very surprised to learn there is a 58 percent chance that such a manager will, in the next fifteen years, underperform his benchmark at least three years in a row.[21] They are even more surprised to learn there is a 27 percent chance that such a manager would underperform for at least four consecutive years over a fifteen-year period.[22]

Imagine that an excellent portfolio manager has a nearly one-third chance of underperforming his benchmark for four consecutive years. The following question reveals a startling statistic, brought to us courtesy of the law of small numbers: What is the probability that our genius manager, who can be expected to beat the market 60 percent of the time over any given one-year period, will be behind the market after fifteen years? Surprisingly, 21 percent of the time our star manager will be trailing slightly after fifteen years even though he can be expected to beat the market during 60 percent of the one-year periods.[23]

Remember, there is no strategy that beats the market 100 percent of the time. A strategy that beats the market 60 percent of the time is a pretty good strategy, but if you abandon a strategy because of poor relative performance alone after a relatively short period, you are committing the mistake of misunderstanding the law of small numbers.

Given the high probability that even very good managers will underperform the market averages for extended periods of time, there is a high probability that investors who evaluate managers solely on performance will not stay with an above-average manager. Fortunately, later in the book we will discuss ways to improve your odds by using SPMs.

6

INTRACTABLE THINKING ERRORS

The next category of limitations in human judgment, intractable thinking errors, discusses errors that appear impossible to fix.

In his book *The Limits of Scientific Reasoning*, David Faust writes:

> Many judgment failings do not result from our having done the wrong thing ... but from our incapacity to do the right thing .... When performing complex judgment tasks, individuals seem incapable of properly weighting more than a few pieces of information.[24]

In this chapter we will discuss thinking errors related to configural analysis and nonlinear relationships between variables.

❏   ❏   ❏

With configural analysis, each new piece of information potentially changes the value of other information. To find the optimal solution to a configural problem, one needs to consider how each piece of information relates to the others.

For example, think about a Rubik's Cube®. Most people can get one side correct with a little practice, but to get all six sides correct at the same time is very difficult. This is because, while you are putting all the squares on the red side together, the blue, orange, yellow, green, and white squares are also moving. So without knowing the solution algorithm, it is almost impossible to know if a twist or a turn will help you solve the puzzle or make it more difficult.

Faust reviewed a number of studies in his book, which supported his contention that human judges are extremely poor at configural reasoning.

In one case he recounts a famous 1972 study, conducted by Hillel Einhorn, looking at survival rates for patients with Hodgkin's disease. In the study three highly trained pathologists were given biopsy slides of 193 deceased patients. They were asked to rate the severity of the disease based on nine characteristics. They were then asked to estimate the patients' survival rates based on the severity ratings.

The pathologists' estimates of the patients' survival rates were extremely inaccurate, with correlation coefficients of .00, +.11 and −.14. The positive correlation coefficient meant that, for that particular pathologist, his prediction rates were inversely correlated with the time the patient lived. In other words, the patients he thought would live the longest died sooner than those he predicted would live the shortest. For the pathologist with the correlation coefficient of .00, his estimates were no better than a random guess.

Einhorn wanted to know if the pathologists' evaluations of the nine characteristics had any predictive value at all. He split the sample size in half and used the first half to develop an SPM based on the evaluations. He then tested the SPM using the other half of the data.

The SPM had a correlation coefficient of −.30, which was more than twice as accurate as the most accurate of the three pathologists.

As Faust points out, the pathologists' judgment of the biopsy slides was indeed useful in making predictions; however, the pathologists were unable to use configural reasoning to combine the data interactively and make useful predictions. As it turned out, the statistical model was more effective at combining the data.

This is similar to the problem faced by a group of nine radiologists studied by P. J. Hoffman and others in 1968, also discussed in Faust's book. The radiologists, asked to differentiate between benign and malignant ulcers in 192 cases, were given up to seven pieces of information. They then examined two-, three-, four-, five-, and six-way interactions among these cues.

Unknown to the group, however, was that there were only 96 distinct cases; each case appeared twice. The researchers did this to determine the consistency of each individual's evaluations.

The results of the study indicated very little consistency among the radiologists. Three pairs of radiologists' evaluations were negatively correlated, suggesting that when one thought a tumor was malignant, the other thought it was benign. Similarly, on the paired cases, the intrasubject test-retest reliability sometimes fell as low as .60, reflecting a low degree of consistency when they evaluated the exact same data twice.

Interestingly, Hoffman and his collaborators tried to develop models that explained the predictions of the radiologists. They found that very simple models summing up the variables explained most of the radiologists' decisions. But more complex models, using configural analysis, ultimately outperformed the radiologists' judgments, demonstrating the intractability of the radiologists' (human judges') task.

Stuart Oskamp's study of the clinical psychologists and psychology students making predictions about Joseph Kidd (discussed earlier in the book) also demonstrated the challenges of configural reasoning. Recall that the test subjects were given four different sets of data and asked the same questions after receiving each new set of data. They were able to change their previous answers based on this new set of data. Part of the reason the psychologists and students did so poorly in their predictions was that they sometimes gave greater weight to new data, despite the fact that it was no more important than the data they already received. They also took data with limited predictability and averaged it with data of high predictability, which acted to dilute the predictive value of the most useful data.

The intractability of this problem was that the test subjects were simply overwhelmed with all sorts of data, some of which was very useful and some of which had little predictive ability regarding Joseph Kidd's personality. They were not able to assign appropriate weights to the data, which is why they predicted so poorly. Nevertheless, the more data they had, the greater confidence they had in their predictions.

❏   ❏   ❏

Another intractable situation for humans is a nonlinear relationship between variables. When there is a linear relationship between variables, increasing one variable will increase the other. For example, if you get paid by the hour, the longer you work, the more you make.

Suppose you and I were standing at a battle monument, watching a nearby jogger. I told you the jogger was moving at a rate of nine feet per second (about six miles per hour) and asked you to estimate how much ground he would cover in 10 seconds, 20 seconds, and 30 seconds. You would answer 90 feet, 180 feet, and 270 feet and wonder why I asked such a simple question.

But let's say I pointed to a cannon on display and asked you the following: If it were to fire a projectile with a muzzle velocity of 2,200 feet per second, how much ground distance would it cover in one second if the angle of elevation on the gun tube were 30 degrees, 45 degrees, and 60 degrees? You might look at me in bewilderment and say you have no idea.[25]

What made the second question appear so much harder than the first? The fact is there is no linear relationship between the angle of elevation of a gun tube and the distance the round will cover in one second. This problem is much different than the linear time-distance problem with the jogger, where the distance traveled increased proportionately to the time elapsed. And when two variables are related but not in a linear fashion (such as distance a projectile travels and gun elevation), humans have more difficulty making accurate predictions.

❏   ❏   ❏

What the gun elevation example and the studies of the radiologists, the pathologists, and the psychologists demonstrate is that sometimes people try to solve problems that are simply too complex for their brains to accomplish.

Security analysis is similarly intractable.

With security analysis, the variables and the price of the stock are in constant motion. It is extremely difficult to calibrate our judgment with so many variables, which can make valuing a company an intractable problem. When we try to do this using our judgment, we may get an estimation, but it is not very likely to be as accurate as if we were to apply statistical prediction methods.

Trying to determine the direction of the stock market is also a highly configural problem with many variables that are not related in a linear fashion. For an individual to reason the market's direction, based on what he reads in the *Wall Street Journal* or sees on CNN is like juggling seven glass balls while spinning in a hula hoop and balancing a stack of china on your head. If you attempt such an intractable juggling challenge, you will end up with glass crashing down all around you.

So, too, if an investor is right about the direction of the market, it is not because he was smart; it is only because he was lucky. But he needs to be on the lookout for his expectations crashing down all around him. Self-deception in the stock market carries its own dangers.

7

CONFIRMATION BIAS PART I

Faust identifies another significant thinking error called confirmation bias. Strictly speaking, this error comes under the category of complex thinking errors.

I decided to give it its own chapter because it is probably the most common complex thinking error an investor can commit. Confirmation bias occurs when people look for ideas that support their preconceived notions and ignore information that is inconsistent with what they believe.

It is our nature as human beings to look for evidence that supports our beliefs. This is why an atheist and a Christian can both look at nature and come to completely opposite conclusions. Have you ever had a friend tell you about an argument with a co-worker? It's all pretty one-sided. As your friend explains, the co-worker was clearly in the wrong. But at the same time, if you were to call your friend's co-worker, you would get an entirely different story.

❏   ❏   ❏

In his book *How We Know What Isn't So,* Thomas Gilovich gives a test that you should try yourself. On a table there are four ordinary index cards. On one card is the letter *A* and on another card is the letter *B*. The other cards are marked 2 and 3.[26]

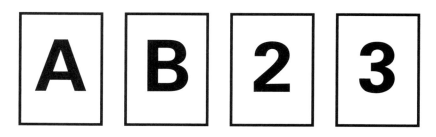

You are given this hypothesis: if there is a vowel on one side of the card, there is an even number on the other side. What cards would you turn over to see if the hypothesis were true? (See the endnote for the correct answer).[27]

If you got the answer right, congratulations! Only a small minority of people answer correctly on the first try. This is because they use confirmation strategies—searching to prove their hypothesis correct. They turn over *A*, thinking they will find an even number, and they turn over *2*, thinking they will find a vowel. What they don't do is turn over *3*, which, if it shows a vowel, would prove the hypothesis false.

If you missed that example of confirmation bias, here is another chance.

In his excellent book *The Black Swan*, Nassim Nicholas Taleb relates an experiment conducted by the psychologist P. C. Wason.[28] Subjects were given a series of numbers, for example:

2, 4, 6

They were then told they should pick the next numbers in the series. The series was created by a rule, and it was the subject's task to determine the rule. After suggesting the next few numbers, they could ask the researcher if the series of numbers were valid. The researcher gave a simple yes or no answer. When the subjects felt confident they knew the rule, they would stop the experiment and announce the rule.

Looking at the series, the most obvious rule is adding two to create the next number. Many people might try:

2, 4, 6, 8, 10, 12

They then would ask the researcher if these numbers were consistent with the rule. The researcher would respond in the affirmative. They then might try the following:

2, 4, 6, 8, 10, 12, 14, 16, 18

They then ask the researcher if this series were correct. The researcher would again answer in the affirmative. Before we go further, let me ask: Are you comfortable at this point concluding that the rule is adding two to the last number?

If you were to guess the next three numbers, what would you guess? Write down your answer and see the endnote for more information on the experiment.[29]

Nassim Nicholas Taleb labels confirmation bias errors of this type **the narrative fallacy.** We observe something and we create an explanation to understand it without ever questioning our explanation.

A recent conversation I had with a very intelligent business-woman demonstrates how confirmation bias can cause us to draw the incorrect conclusions about our investment approaches.

As this woman explained to me, she knew virtually nothing about the stock market until she heard some friends talking about how well they were doing. She began studying the market, reading the *Wall Street Journal* and several business magazines, and buying stocks on her own through a discount broker.

The stocks went up, and she concluded that she was an excellent stock picker. Her logic went something like this: "I am a very intelligent, highly educated person with excellent judgment. I make excellent decisions in other areas of my life because of my intelligence and education. I can do the same in the stock market."

She believed that by reading the popular financial magazines and newspapers, she could outperform the market on a fairly consistent basis. In effect, she made up a narrative or story to explain why she was doing so well in the market. Eventually, she got very busy with her profession and no longer had the time to do the research. She turned the stock selection over to a broker whose performance was much worse.

This example shows exactly how confirmation bias works. This woman wanted an explanation for why the stocks she bought were doing so well. She found a convenient explanation in her belief in her excellent judgment.

What she never did was to test any **disconfirmation strategies.** She could also have said, "Technology stocks are in a bull market now, and they are all over the news. Most of what I read is about technology stocks, and perhaps this is just a short window when I can make money buying the stocks in the news."

Or she could have said, "I have been studying the stock market rather intensely for only a few months. Other people have studied it for their whole careers. Perhaps the reason I did so well with my stock purchases is that I just got lucky. I will have to see much more evidence before I conclude that I am a great stock picker."

Indeed, she never considered explanations for her success that were not consistent with her preconceived idea. Certainly it is possible that the cause of her success was luck or just being in a bull market.

Here is the ironic part: this highly educated, intelligent businesswoman was a psychologist. In the course of her education, she had no doubt studied confirmation bias and other decision-making errors. She was familiar with the scientific method and hypothesis testing. No doubt, if a patient of hers were suffering from confirmation bias affecting his interpersonal relationships, she would understand this and make appropriate recommendations. But when it came to her own decision making, she was blind to the bias.

This story illustrates how pervasive, insidious, and ubiquitous confirmation bias is. Simply being aware of it, or even having studied it intently, is not always enough to avoid it in our own judgment-based decision making.

As a tournament chess player, I have seen confirmation bias on a regular basis in my own games and the games of others. Chess players conduct an internal dialogue during games and draw conclusions about their positions.

Many times after the game, players will discuss key points and frequently will have very different opinions about the positions.

These differences are frequently caused by the player's desire to believe the game is going well and that he, not his opponent, has the advantage.

It can be very amusing to watch the discussion that takes place after the game when one player suggests he had a decisive advantage and his opponent argues that the position was equal. The one constant is that players never underestimate their positions during the postmortem analysis. Both sides tend to overestimate their own positions.

The combination of overconfidence and confirmation bias frequently is the underlying cause of blunders that can cost the game. The result is that while good chess players rarely miss opportunities on the board for themselves, most players below Grandmaster level find they overlook good moves for their opponents far more frequently.

The tendency to overlook an opponent's ideas is insidious. I know this and have even conducted training exercises to rid my own games of this error. Yet despite all the efforts I put into avoiding confirmation bias, I still find these types of errors seep into my thinking and cause me to lose games I should not have lost. Like most humans, I sometimes fail to do the things I know I should.

Perhaps this is the reason world-renowned chess coach Mark Dvoretsky teaches his students to avoid confirmation biases by beginning their thinking not by asking, "What should I do now?" but by asking, "If I could pass the move to my opponent, what would he do next?"

❏   ❏   ❏

As investors, we have an advantage that tournament chess players do not have. We can use a statistical model to select our securities.

The only surefire strategy for avoiding confirmation bias with individual stock selection is to stick rigidly to naked portfolio manager strategies that do not require you to interject your judgment into the decision-making process.

$$\boxed{8}$$

Confirmation Bias Part II

So as not to be guilty of confirmation bias ourselves, we examine several challenges to our thesis that investment results will improve when we use our judgment to select appropriate *statistical prediction methods* instead of appropriate *securities.*

❏ ❏ ❏

The first challenge we will address holds that **decision making in the stock market is "different."**

With all human decision making, the decision maker brings his emotions, biases, heuristics, life experiences, and human frailties to a set of facts and makes a prediction. In the previously discussed studies of statistical prediction, whether the prediction is about recidivism, heart disease, success in medical school, or Supreme Court rulings, models that outperformed individuals' judgment-based predictions were constructed.

From my experience and research, this reasoning holds true for the stock market as well. Indeed, the majority of mutual funds are managed by individuals applying their own judgment, and not surprisingly, the majority underperform the S&P 500. Stock market SPMs are no different than decision-making models for other disciplines, which are created by analyzing years of data then applied in a disciplined, consistent manner.

❏　　❏　　❏

The next challenge to SPMs contends that **all stock information is immediately priced** and there is no advantage to gain by analyzing historical data to make future predictions.

The problem with this argument is that it does not take into account the difference between *information* and *knowledge.*

Information is indeed immediately priced in the market, especially when reported in the media. For example, if a company announces surprisingly good earnings after the close, its stock frequently goes up immediately in after-hours trading. Investors who buy stock the next morning at the opening bell will then be too late to take advantage of the news.

Knowledge, however, is something that gets priced much more slowly. Here's an illustration. In 1949 Ben Graham, in his popular book *The Intelligent Investor,* advised purchasing stocks for less than their net working capital. He was referring to securities with prices so low that if the company took all its cash and paid off all its debt and distributed the remaining cash, shareholders would receive more in cash than they paid for the stock.

Even though this was a widely read book, the types of stocks it touted remained available for years.[30] While readers of the book had the opportunity to profit from this knowledge, few did so because the investing public responds much more slowly to new knowledge about markets than it does to new information about stocks.

Another example of the market failing to price new knowledge quickly is shown by the response to Ken Fisher's 1984 book *Super Stocks,* which made the case that investors could improve their stock selections by using price-to-sales ratios.

For the next ten years, the price-to-sales ratio served as a useful tool for identifying winning stocks, according to Fisher. But at some point, the knowledge became widely accepted, readily available information. By the time his 2007 book, *The Only Three Questions That Count,* was published, he suggested there was no longer much of an advantage to using price-to-sales ratios because so many people were using them.[31]

❏   ❏   ❏

One popular argument against the use of SPMs says that a **small number of extraordinary professionals are truly gifted at picking stocks and their gifts cannot be encapsulated in a model.**

On the contrary, with what we know from the Kasparov–Deep Blue match, we can make the case that SPMs created by great masters (such as gifted stock pickers) would actually outperform the masters themselves because the SPMs would be more consistent.

Furthermore, if you seek only portfolio managers with long-established records of beating the market handsomely and select only those with outstanding records, you will likely find that those individuals will be managing such huge portfolios that it may handicap their ability to beat the market.

Peter Lynch said in his book *One Up on Wall Street* that his biggest disadvantage was the size of his portfolio (the well-known Magellan fund, which experienced huge returns under his direction).

Lynch suggested that individual investors had significant advantages over professional managers with huge portfolios:

> The bigger the equity fund, the harder it gets for it to outperform the competition. Expecting a $9-billion fund to compete successfully against an $800-million fund is the same as expecting Larry Bird to star in basketball games with a five pound weight strapped to his waist. Big funds have the same built-in handicaps as big anythings—the bigger it is, the more energy it takes to move it.[32]

Shortly after the book was written, Lynch quit. While Fidelity no doubt tried to find the very best talent for its flagship mutual fund, Lynch's successors fared much worse than he did. It could have been because they were less talented than Lynch or because the mammoth size of the fund made it impossible to get meaningful positions in the small, undervalued companies that Lynch was able to buy when the fund was much smaller.

In light of the Magellan experience, selecting and implementing high-quality SPMs may be a much safer strategy for the individual investor than chasing fund performance.

❏   ❏   ❏

The most serious challenge to SPMs is the **efficient market hypothesis,** which suggests that because all information about stocks is known and priced, investors cannot use information to gain an advantage in the marketplace.

My reason for rejecting this theory is unconventional and, I believe, compelling: if this hypothesis were true of the stock market, then it should be true of other "decision/risk markets" where individuals make bets on future outcomes.

Yet this is not the case. There are many examples of inefficient markets. Studies of Major League Baseball draft picks and Internet poker, for example, show that individuals do not always make optimal decisions and that process inefficiencies can be exploited.

Let's look at baseball, probably the most competitive decision/ risk market around. All the teams strive each year to get the best talent in the draft. But many of the less financially endowed, small-market teams argue that the draft process is unfair to them because they do not have enough money to attract the best talent away from the wealthier, large-market teams.

But one small-market team, the Oakland Athletics, with a budget less than a third of that of the largest market team, has a record of consistently producing excellent teams.

The story of their success is chronicled in the best-selling 2003 book *Moneyball* by Michael Lewis. He makes the case that the market for baseball players is very inefficient. Indeed, while wealthier teams frequently pay exorbitant amounts for players, teams such as the A's find the talented players overlooked by the majority of the Major League teams.

THEIR SECRET? SPMS.

Lewis describes how SPMs contributed to the team's successes, explaining that, with a budget for ballplayers that was the second lowest in baseball, the A's won 91 games in 2000 and an astonishing 102 games in 2001 (for nonbaseball fans, the regular season is 162 games).[33]

Here's how it came about. Back in the seventies, an obscure baseball fan named Bill James developed a number of theories about baseball, self-publishing them in a little-read publication called *1977 Baseball Abstract: Featuring 18 Categories of Statistical Information That You Just Can't Find Anywhere Else.*

One of James's theories challenged baseball's mainstream view of a player's ability to draw walks, generally thought to require no skill.

James realized, in fact, that drawing walks did require an important skill—to *not* swing at bad pitches. He also discovered that players with extraordinarily small strike zones drew a lot more walks. And a team that drew a lot of walks, all other things being equal, scored more runs and won more games.

Billy Beane, the general manager of the Oakland A's, was a fan of James's theory and used it in selecting players. Unlike most managers, Beane paid less attention to the traditional metric of batting average, which excluded walks. Instead, he focused more on players' on-base percentage (which included walks in the calculation). As a result, he sometimes chose short, fat players (with small strike zones) who nobody else wanted, thus taking advantage of inefficient pricing in the baseball player market and leading his team to unprecedented success.

James's influence has spread. In 2002 the Red Sox hired him to help them implement his SPMs. After an eighty-six-year drought, the team won the World Series in 2004 and again in 2007.[34]

Another example of a decision/risk market is poker. If this market were truly efficient, no one could win in the long run. In the stock market, according to the efficient market hypothesis, everything is known. Therefore, stocks cannot trade at bargain prices because no one would ever sell a stock for less than it was worth.

By analogy, in poker, everything about the theory of the game is known and published. Therefore, good poker players will always make the theoretically correct play. In addition, all poker players must be losers eventually because the house or Internet site removes a small percentage from each pot.

Of course, we know that, while most poker players are losers in the long run, a small percentage of poker players make a living at the game. This is because not everyone knows or applies the correct poker theory all the time, and in this decision/risk market, a few elite players are consistent winners over time by making better decisions than most players.

I believe that the baseball and poker analogies are applicable to the stock market. Even though the stock market is very difficult to beat, a select group of individuals will be able to prevail over the long term because they will make better decisions than most other investors. Individuals who employ SPMs have the best chances of being in that select group.

9

HOW THINKING ERRORS SABOTAGE
YOUR INVESTMENT RETURNS

Most people don't even realize they make errors in their decision making, yet the results of the errors I've discussed cost investors billions.

❑   ❑   ❑

To give you another idea of how thinking errors sabotage mutual fund investors, take a look at the chart on the following page from DALBAR, a highly respected, Boston-based research firm that studies many aspects of mutual fund performance and investor behavior. The chart illustrates how real-world investors frequently get it wrong when timing mutual fund transactions.

As you can see, over the twenty-year period ending in 2006, the average return of the S&P Index was 11.9 percent, but the return of the average equity mutual fund investor was only 3.9 percent; in other words, mutual fund investors underperformed the market by 8 percent per year. Yet if you look at the returns quoted by most mutual fund families, their equity funds returns are normally much better.

Most investors, in fact, do not understand that there is a difference between the funds' returns and the individual investors' returns.

DALBAR STUDY OF MUTUAL FUND INVESTOR RETURNS

Category	Annualized Return 1986–2005	Annualized Return 1987–2006	Change
S&P 500 Index	11.9%	11.8%	−0.1%
Average Equity Fund Investor	3.9%	4.3%	+0.4%
Average Fixed Income Fund Investor	1.8%	1.7%	−0.1%
Average Asset Allocation Investor	3.3%	3.7%	+0.4%
Average Systematic Equity Investor	6.0%	6.1%	+0.1%
Average Equity Market Timer	−2.1%	−1.8%	+0.3%

35

Let me illustrate with an example. Suppose you walk into your broker's office and tell her you have saved $10,000 that you want to invest in a mutual fund. She suggests you buy the Paolucci Aggressive Growth Fund at $10 per share.

You invest your $10,000, purchasing 1,000 shares. One year later the share price has increased to $20, and your investment has doubled. You are elated when your broker calls you to give you the good news. You tell her how happy you are and that your wife has just inherited $980,000 from her Aunt Matilda. You told your wife that you knew exactly the place for her inheritance— the Paolucci Aggressive Growth Fund.

Your broker takes the order and buys you 49,000 shares of the fund at $20 per share. A year later the fund has dropped to $14 per share, and your wife is apoplectic about how you could be so stupid as to lose so much of the money Aunt Matilda had saved. You go see your broker, and she says, "I don't know why you are upset. The fund is up 40 percent in two years."

This example shows the difference between **dollar-weighted returns** and **time-weighted returns.** In the example the investor's dollar-weighted return is down almost 30 percent while the fund is up 20 percent per year. The share price of the Paolucci Aggressive Growth Fund is up 40 percent from $10 per share to $14 dollars per share.

You made two purchases of the fund: you have $10,000 invested for two years at a simple rate of 20 percent per year, and you have $980,000 invested for one year at a rate of −30 percent per year. The fact that almost all of your money was invested at the peak means that your dollar-weighted return is determined much more by the return of the $980,000 than the return of the $10,000.

Indeed, for many mutual funds, the average return of the mutual fund itself is substantially higher than the average return of an investor's holdings in the same fund.

How that can be? Much of the difference comes from **poor market timing decisions** by investors (largely caused by the decision-making errors discussed in the previous chapters).

While it is true that most core equity funds have trailed the S&P 500 over ten-year periods, the huge difference in return is not caused by fund underperformance alone. The fact is, individual investors as a group are terrible market timers. They tend to pour money into funds at the top of the market and pull money out after things have gone down considerably.

But we know why. Individual investors and some portfolio managers do not understand these important concepts:

- The rule of short time periods: With investing, the longer we invest, the more likely our return will approach the expected return for the asset class in which we invest. When investors invest for very short time periods, the chances their returns will be substantially different than the long-term average is considerably higher.

- The rule of small numbers: This is the same principle we studied with the two hospitals in which the one that had only fifteen children born each day was much more likely to deviate from the norm (half boys and half girls) than the hospital that delivered forty-five babies.

When the market is going gangbusters, greed gets the best of individual investors, and they can't wait to get in. When things start to go down, they look for a reason to get out of the market. The media will always be available to give them a host of justifications to get out of a falling market.

The DALBAR study shows how the rule of short time periods works in conjunction with faulty confirmation strategies to cause investors to sabotage their own strategies. If they select a fund and it appreciates nicely, they will seldom ask, "Is anything wrong with my fund's strategy?" When the inevitable bumpy period hits, the rule of short time periods can cause them to search for a reason for the underperformance and abandon the strategy.

❑   ❑   ❑

Here is more evidence that investors are sabotaging their invest-ment strategies. The chart below shows six widely held mutual funds and compares the investors' returns to the funds' returns. As you can see, over the ten-year period, the shareholders' returns lagged behind the funds' returns by anywhere from 2 percent to more than 14 percent. The most amazing statistic here is that even the investors in the S&P 500 index fund underperformed the S&P 500 fund by 2 percent per year.

GROWTH FUND RETURNS VERSUS INVESTOR RETURNS:
AGGRESSIVE GROWTH FUNDS, 1995–2005

Fund Group Overall Manager	Annual Return				
	1995–2000 Total	2000–2005 Total	10-Year Fund	10-Year Shareholder	10-Year Shareholder Lag
Alliance Bernstein Growth	20.1%	−5.2%	6.7%	−7.6%	−14.3%
Fidelity Growth	21.6	−2.5	8.8	3.4	−5.5
Janus Growth	21.8	−3.3	9.8	1.4	−8.5
MFS Growth	20.7	−4.6	7.3	−1.1	−8.4
Putnam Growth	17.8	−3.7	6.5	1.7	−4.8
Average	21.0%	−3.9%	7.8%	−0.5%	−8.3%
Vanguard Index 500	18.4%	0.5%	9.1%	7.1%	−2.0%

36

What we can learn from this chart is that investor behavior is sometimes much more important than investment performance. Instead of worrying about what is the best fund, mutual fund investors should think about what funds they would be comfortable holding for extended periods of time.

These charts tell us that investors are making emotional market calls that are destroying their ability to create wealth. It turns out that investor behavior is more important than the mutual fund vehicle they select.

PART III

Putting Statistical Prediction
Methods into Practice

Introduction:
Why Portfolio Managers Don't Use SPMs

Traditional portfolio managers would have us believe that what really matters most is their judgment. They will protest that what they know from their training, experience, and intuition cannot be distilled into a model; investing is too complicated for that.

Many traditional judgment-based portfolio managers look with contempt on "quant" (short for quantitative)-based portfolio managers, who feed all kinds of data into the computer and the mysterious "black box" spits out information they study to make their investing decisions.

Traditional portfolio managers are also "black box" technicians but of a different kind. They feed all types of information into their brains, and *poof*—out comes a decision. The black box is in their heads, and transforming their judgments to a clear box for the entire world to see—to manage their portfolios nakedly—is very scary for them.

Indeed, fear is one of the two primary reasons statistical prediction methods are not in widespread use.

The idea that a simple set of rules, strictly applied and rigidly followed, can provide a better result than their judgment certainly threatens these traditional portfolio managers, possibly because most of them can't beat the market averages consistently. Remember, these people are being paid hundreds of thousands of dollars—sometimes millions of dollars—a year to believe they are in the minority who can beat the market.

As a group, portfolio managers are extremely bright and tremendously overconfident. It is easy to rationalize underperformance. The market provides plenty of opportunity to blame everyone and everything, including the Federal Reserve chair, the price of oil, other analysts, and even the weather.

The fact is to beat the market long term, the most important thing is the portfolio manager's ability to make decisions that are significantly better than those of his peers. This ability is very rare.

Another reason SPMs are not in widespread use is financial. For more than a hundred years, Wall Street has been selling advice. Firms compete to manage money, and the main ways to compete in sales are through exclusivity and competitive advantage. For example, if you want Midas Moneymaker to manage your portfolio, you have to buy the Moneymaker funds, offered only by Wanamaker Securities, members of the NYSE.

But portfolios based on SPMs can be easily replicated by the competition and can be managed inexpensively. There is no need for highly compensated research analysts and, thus, no justification for high management fees. Therefore, fund companies have little financial incentive to embrace an SPM approach.

SPMs today remind me of life insurance forty years ago. When people bought this type of insurance when I was growing up, they usually bought whole life insurance. You got protection for your family, and the policy accumulated cash value you could borrow against or use some day.

Cheaper term life insurance was available, but agents and insurance companies focused on the whole life product. No one liked term insurance because you got nothing in return unless you died, and premiums got more expensive as you got older. Insurance companies and their agents encouraged people to buy whole life because it was a very profitable product.

Eventually consumers wised up. They realized they could get a lot more protection for less money if they purchased term insurance. Furthermore, they realized they could invest their own money more profitably than giving it to the insurance company to invest for them in a whole life policy. "Buy term and invest the difference" became the mantra.

Maybe one day investors will say, "Use statistical prediction methods and invest the difference." We will see.

It is important to note here that I do not in any way think whole life insurance or mutual funds are bad. Nothing could be further from the truth. Whole life definitely has its place, especially in estate planning. And I think mutual funds are terrific wealth accumulation vehicles that allow individuals to get small amounts of money managed in diversified portfolios through monthly investments. Mutual funds, while appropriate for 401(k) and other retirement-type investments, have a poor rate of return relative to the market. Affluent investors should avoid chasing fund performance and instead use statistical prediction.

10

SEEING THINGS IN A NEW WAY

"Dad, if God did not want Adam and Eve to eat from the apple tree, why didn't he put a fence around it?

"Actually, Dad, why did he put the tree there in the first place?"

—Abigail Fischer, age 7

Abigail's questions poignantly illustrate the type of thinking we are capable of when our minds are unconstrained by years of dogmatic teaching. We have been taught all our lives that the story of Adam and Eve is about Man's fall from grace when he commits the original sin.

Abigail's bright, young mind is wide open and, thus, asks the entirely plausible question as to whether the story is about God's failure to protect his children from the evil serpent who would lead them astray. Of course, the idea that God is fallible is not in the lexicon of religious speech. Abigail does not yet understand this. She is not being blasphemous; she is merely thinking critically.

For years, the mutual fund industry has preached the gospel of the superiority of professional management. Individual investors and stock brokers have been taught by the fund industry that they are foolish to buy stocks themselves. Why buy stocks when you can get this brilliant portfolio manager, a graduate of one of the most prestigious schools in the country, with a team of analysts that visits hundreds of companies every year, to buy stocks for you? The implication is that he can do it better than you can. And the fact is that he probably can do it better than you can if you try to make decisions the same way as he does.

But you do not have to make decisions that way; you can use SPMs.

Accepting the premise that actuarial models outperform human judgment should change your thinking. Instead of focusing on what stocks to buy or what investment magazine to read, your thinking goes to what variables are important in the construction of an actuarial model. It goes to the books you read, the research you review. It changes everything about your approach.

Once you have decided that actuarial strategies give you the best opportunity to beat the market averages, you need to decide how best to select and implement your strategies.

We learned in the section discussing the rule of small numbers that if a strategy has a 60 percent chance of beating the market in any given year, there is better than a 6 percent chance the strategy will underperform the market in the first three years that it is implemented and almost a 3 percent chance the strategy will trail the market during each of the first four years it is implemented.

If we all thought super-logically, as does Spock on *Star Trek,* this would not affect us. We would continue to follow the strategy, confident that eventually the law of averages would work out for us and, after enough time, mean regression would occur and our portfolio would be ahead of the market.

But we don't think super-logically, and I know from experience that many clients do not have the emotional fortitude to stick with a fundamentally sound strategy for even four months of underperformance, let alone four years.

This is why the DALBAR study shows how mutual fund investors underperform the funds in which they invest. Investors do not understand the law of small numbers or its corollary, the rule of short time periods, and quickly abandon funds or strategies without giving them enough time to work out.

So the question then arises, how can we reduce the risk that our emotions will get the best of us and cause us to lapse into bad investment thinking habits? How can we keep from abandoning SPMs when we have the inevitable period of underperformance every investor faces at some time? We can do this by combining actuarial strategies with behavioral strategies.

First, look at what happens if you use four **actuarial strategies** instead of just one. Let's assume that each strategy has a 60 percent chance of beating your benchmark, and for the purposes of this discussion, let's assume that all four strategies perform independently of each other.

That is to say, if strategy A underperforms its benchmark, strategy B, strategy C, and strategy D still have a 60 percent likelihood of outperforming their benchmarks.

If you equally weight the strategies and assume that the percentage of change, up or down, is the same for each strategy, then the probability of underperforming your benchmark after one year drops to just 18 percent. The probability you will underperform for two consecutive years is only a little more than 3 percent. (There is a 35 percent chance each year you will have two models ahead of the market and two models behind.)

Now for some real-world practicalities. First, we are never going to know if any given strategy has a 60 percent chance of beating a benchmark over a given year. Next, if we pick our strategies carefully, they are not likely to be completely uncorrelated to each other and, thus, not 100 percent independent, as I have assumed above. And finally, the percentage of change up or down for each strategy will not be the same.

Nevertheless, the statistical point is clear: by using a multiplicity of effective actuarial strategies, we reduce the risk of significantly underperforming our benchmarks.

❏   ❏   ❏

Now let's talk about some behavioral strategies. To be a successful investor, you must manage your money and manage your emotions.

Many people are unsuccessful at managing their emotions when it comes to investments. Therefore, it is helpful to have a partner with a long-term perspective. This is why you may want to work with a financial advisor who can help you implement the strategies.

Granted, you can implement the strategies yourself, but it is very easy to get off track. A financial advisor should act as a coach to keep you pursuing your strategies, even when you go through a difficult period in the market.

While it is possible to implement statistical strategies without a coach, you really have to know yourself well. Human nature being what it is, it is very easy to get sidetracked. If you want to implement SPMs yourself, you may want to get a partner such as your spouse or a trusted friend to schedule periodic reviews to make sure you are implementing the strategies in a consistent and disciplined manner. We know that investors' behavior frequently sabotages them in down markets. Having a good coach is the best insurance against this.

It is important to remember what we have learned about the law of small numbers and the rule of short time periods. Let's say we have carefully selected three actuarial strategies, and after three years, two have been working well and one has trailed the market. That is not the time to liquidate the underperforming strategy and put the money into the other strategies. To recognize when we need to change a strategy, we need to look beyond performance.

❏   ❏   ❏

So when do we change an SPM? What if one of your SPMs has underperformed for a period of time?

First, remember that Rule One is that SPMs are used to develop a broadly diversified, equally weighted portfolio that is sector neutral or at the very least diversified into several different market sectors. It is almost never correct to abandon a *correctly selected* SPM *on performance alone.*

Therefore, it is important to examine the reasons you selected that particular SPM:

- Was it based on reliable data?
- Was it based on sound, empirically researched assumptions?
- Are you using an appropriate benchmark when measuring performance? For example, if you compare the SPM to the S&P 500 after large capitalization stocks have done very well, few equally weighted multicap strategies will compare favorably.

It will be helpful to look back to analogous time periods when the SPM also trailed the market.

Let's say, for example, you have decided to use the Dogs of the Dow, a very simple SPM in which you invest equal amounts of money into the ten Dow stocks with the highest yield and rebalance your portfolio annually for your large capitalization exposure. Let's say after three years of using this strategy, you have trailed the market for three straight years. You are not sure, but you think it might have something to do with rising energy prices. It is very easy to look back and see if there were periods in history when the strategy trailed for three consecutive years. You can also see how the strategy did during the 1973–74 oil embargo. You should look back and study the strategy following three years of underperformance or after a period of sharply rising energy prices.

In contrast, the investor who uses traditional methods frequently does not have a historical tool to measure his manager against. His portfolio manager may have been managing money for only a short time period, and while there is an analogous period in history to review, it would not be possible to see how the manager did during the 1973–74 oil embargo because he was not managing money then. Maybe he was in Cub Scouts or he wasn't even born yet.

❑   ❑   ❑

This brings up another key point about naked strategies. All well-constructed naked strategies are designed to capitalize on the psychological mistakes of other investors (as described in chapters 4 through 7). Driven by fear and greed, humans continue to make errors in judgment. But because naked strategies don't change or evolve, history can provide some insight useful for evaluating an SPM.

Humans do evolve. They get older, learn, forget, get passionate about the market, lose their passion for the market, fall in love, fall out of love, have children, take up golf, quit golf, get rich, get fat, get lazy, lose weight, and rededicate themselves to their work. They are changing all the time.

Many portfolio managers begin their careers working seventy hours a week, studying trade journals, reading research, visiting management, building cash flow models, and feeding their brains with all types of facts they use to develop their inner "black boxes." But few people are able to keep up this pace for their entire careers. And when the pace slows for any variety of reasons, the magic of the box can wane.

But this does not happen to the naked portfolio manager.

If one of the SPMs you are using trails badly for an extended period, you will have to use your judgment (yes, I am really saying this) to determine if you have made a mistake in selecting a poor SPM. Please keep in mind all the judgment traps we have discussed and be loath to change an SPM. If keeping money in a strategy that appears sound but has been trailing badly for a period of time is too painful to do emotionally, then consider reducing the percentage you have in that strategy.

The above assumes that your personal financial situation remains the same. If your Aunt Matilda leaves you a fortune or your twin high school boys sign multiyear contracts with the Yankees or you lose your job, it is certainly acceptable to consider changes to your SPMs to adapt to the new situation.

STATISTICAL PREDICTION METHODS IN PRACTICE

In this chapter we will look at four thoroughly researched prediction tools that practitioners use to create statistical prediction models. These strategies are logical, based on sound economic principles, and extremely robust.

Remember, to properly use statistical prediction, your portfolio selection rules must be clearly defined so anyone using those rules would create the same portfolio. If your rules are ambiguous, you run the risk of interjecting your judgment into the model and, with it, human error.

❏   ❏   ❏

THE CRIPPS VALUE REVERSION EQUITY COMPASS

The Cripps Value Reversion Equity Compass is an excellent example of an SPM that can be used to construct a portfolio with superb chances of producing very satisfactory portfolio returns.

This SPM was developed by Richard Cripps with the assistance of Timothy McCann in the fall of 2001, while they were employed at a regional brokerage firm. The Compass was designed to give advisors a statistically based tool for managing portfolios.

The logical basis of the model rests on three very plausible assumptions:

1. Most of the time, most stocks are fairly priced.

2. Sometimes some stocks are mispriced.

3. Stocks are more likely to be mispriced at extremes, rather than in their normal price range.

All three of these assumptions are inherently logical.

We believe the first assumption is correct because within a distribution of stock returns, we see that the returns of individual stocks are clustered around the average for the market itself.

The second assumption appears to be true also. Every year there are stocks that provide fantastic returns and stocks that decline substantially. Sometimes the cause of these extreme returns is a random event that no one could foresee, such as the effect of the 2001 terrorist attacks on cruise industry stocks. But other times these outsized returns are caused by extreme valuations created by investor overreaction, such as Internet stocks in early 2000 or energy stocks in the 1980s.

Finally, the last assumption seems to be consistent with the principle of regression to the mean.

Believing their assumptions correct, Cripps and his team set out to create a model to identify when stock prices, relative to their underlying fundamentals, were at extreme valuations.

Creating this model was a daunting task. Just because a stock was down in price was no reason to believe it was mispriced. For example, some stocks undergo a permanent revaluation due to a fundamental change in their business. After all, if a company with a longtime successful business model selling encyclopedias door-to-door was trading at historic low valuations, it could be because the stock was cheap, or it could be because somebody invented the CD-ROM, a substitute product that sold for $39.95, replacing the $1,500 encyclopedia.

So Cripps and his team created a tool that told them when a stock was mispriced based not on historic valuations, but on forward-looking estimates relative to the market.

In a December 2005 research piece, Cripps explained the methodology as follows:

> Our analysis starts by determining where each stock falls on the basis of valuation relative to a broader universe of stocks (approximately 1600). Each stock is scored on a scale from 0% to 100%. Lower scores are classified as "value" and higher scores are viewed as "growth." Stocks with a relative valuation score of 50% are considered "market average."[37]

These scores are computed by ranking each stock separately on forward-looking valuation measures that include ratios such as price to earnings, price to cash flow, price to sales, and price to growth rate. A composite score is then computed by averaging the scores in each of the fundamental categories.

Next the scores are converted to a percentile rating. This percentile score is used to create a synthetic price. For example, if you asked where Caterpillar was trading, you could say $66 dollar per share, or you could say 24 percent (the valuation relative to all other stocks).

By measuring the change in synthetic price, you could measure how the market was changing the value it placed on Caterpillar's fundamentals, relative to other stocks in the market.

Stocks with the greatest decrease in their synthetic price, relative to their twelve-month average, were the stocks most likely to be mispriced.

Cripps tested his model by calculating the average of the synthetic prices for the past twelve months of each of the stocks in the database and contrasting that average with the stocks' scores for the current month.

If his model worked, stocks substantially below their twelve-month average should outperform other stocks in the market because their prices reflected extreme investor overreaction.

Cripps called the difference between the twelve-month score and the current score the mean value discount (MVD) and contrasted the returns of the stocks with the greatest MVDs with the market as a whole. He called stocks with MVDs in the bottom 10 percent of the database "redline" stocks.

The results of Cripps's analysis are shown below.

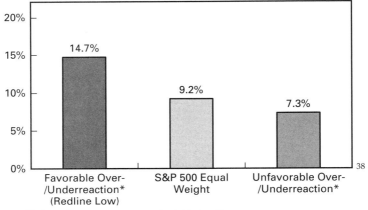

AGGREGATE PERFORMANCE OF STOCKS
EXPERIENCING INVESTOR OVER-/UNDERREACTION

Annualized Performances (6/28/02–1/31/08)

* Index performances assume equal-weighted positions
rebalanced and reconstituted monthly.
Dividends excluded.
Source: Stifel Nicolaus Portfolio Strategy Group

As you can see from the table, the redline *low* stocks, represented by the far left column, outperformed the market as a whole on an equal-weighted basis. These stocks, designated favorable over-/underreaction, were the stocks whose price relative to value dropped the most from their twelve-month value.

The stocks in the far right column, designated unfavorable over-/underreaction, were the stocks that had the lowest returns and whose prices were the most above the twelve-month average.

Cripps explains the stellar performance of the redline stocks this way:

> Traditional approaches to identifying mispriced stocks are premised on doing deep analysis to identify intrinsic value error. As with any [judgment-based] intrinsic value analysis, the judgment involved [with] looking into the future is fraught with all kinds of intended and unintended bias. The Equity Compass identifies mispriced stocks

by systematically quantifying changes in investor behavior (as expressed by the stock price) and investors' expectations (as expressed in common valuation measure such as price to earnings, price to cash flow, etc.).[39]

It appears that Cripps's model is capitalizing on two cognitive errors.

The first is investor overreaction, which occurs when a stock's fundamentals deteriorated, but investors push the stock price too low relative to the valuations they had been placing on the stock in the past year. This could occur when the stock's earnings cash flow and/or sales decline (or fail to grow as quickly as Wall Street expects) and investors dump the stock, pushing the price down too far in relation to the disappointing fundamentals.

The other cognitive error Cripps's model addresses is anchoring. This can occur when a stock has traded in a range for a long period of time and investors are reluctant to push the stock out of its current trading range despite the fact that the fundamentals are very strong. Investors become anchored on the top of the range and refuse to pay more for the stock.

But stocks don't stay underpriced forever, and eventually other, unanchored investors become attracted to the stock and push it through the top of its trading range.

Note that Cripps's model is highly configural. Each new piece of information affects the weight we assign to the other variables. With this SPM, if you know that the stock's current synthetic price is 38 percent, you know nothing, but if you know that its average for the past twelve months has been 58 percent, making it a redline stock, you know much more.

Remember that humans are really bad at configural thinking. This tool gives investors information about how the market is valuing a company now and in the recent past—information they could not know intuitively. The model's excellent results capitalize on the pricing errors of other investors.

❏   ❏   ❏

THE JEREMY SIEGEL MODEL

This next SPM, which deals with the world of indexing, was developed by Professor Jeremy Siegel, the Russell E. Palmer Professor of Finance at the Wharton School of the University of Pennsylvania. He received his PhD from MIT and is the author of the best-selling book *Stocks for the Long Run.*

Indexes are groups of stocks selected by a committee and designed to communicate information about the market and the U.S. economy. The most famous index is the S&P 500, which is a group of 500 large-capitalization companies considered leading companies in leading industries. Equity managers are frequently compared to this index.

In his book, Siegel identifies some of the shortcomings of traditional indexing, including something he calls the "entry premium." This refers to the tendency for stocks to rise after the announcement that they will be included in the S&P 500. Investors in index funds pay substantially higher prices for stocks after the announcement but prior to the date they are actually added.

One extreme example was Yahoo! After the close on November 30, 1999, Standard & Poor's announced it would add Yahoo! to the S&P 500 on December 7. Yahoo! rose 64 percent in the next five days, causing index investors to pay top dollar to get the stock.

The S&P 500 is a capitalization-weighted index, which means that all 500 stocks in the index are not weighted equally. A company such as Exxon Mobil, with a market capitalization of almost $500 billion, has much more impact on the index than does a company such as Manitowoc, with a market capitalization of $5 billion.

Although each year S&P makes a few changes to the portfolio, the fact that the index is capitalization weighted means there is never any requirement to rebalance the stocks in the S&P 500. That is, if the index were equally weighted, meaning that an equal dollar amount was placed in each stock, Standard & Poor's would have to make adjustments at periodic intervals to bring the index back into balance with the same number of dollars in each stock.

Siegel believed that an intelligent rebalancing approach might be an effective strategy to enhance the return of an index. He reasoned that if you sold shares of stock when they were high and used the money to buy shares of stock when they were low, you would be able to take advantage of the natural fluctuations of stock prices to enhance return. He also knew that a substantial part of the return of the stock market came from dividends. Therefore, he suggested that dividend weighting might make for an index that produced higher returns than a capitalization-weighted index.

In a dividend-weighted index, the percentage of capital allocated to a stock depends on the dividend rate and the number of shares outstanding. Also, a dividend-weighted index must be periodically rebalanced. When that occurs, capital is reallocated toward stocks whose yield has increased (because the share price is down or because the dividend has been boosted). Shares of stocks with substantial price increases and without increased dividends are typically sold to buy shares of cheaper, better yielding stocks.

In a chart prepared for WisdomTree Investments, Inc., (seen on the following page), Siegel compared the performance of dividend-weighted indexes to capitalization-weighted indexes in four market segments.

RISK AND RETURN CHARACTERISTICS
OF WISDOM TREE DOMESTIC INDEXES
January 1, 1964 to May 31, 2006 — Based on a Hypothetical Back Test

Market Segment	Index	Avg. Annual Total Return	Annualized Volatility	Sharpe Ratio	BETA
Total Market	**Wisdom Tree Dividend Index**	**11.88%**	**13.29%**	**0.524**	**0.851**
	Hypothetical Reference Index—Total Market	10.62%	15.10%	0.396	1.015
	Gain Relative to Hypothetical Reference Index	126 bps	−181 bps	0.128	−0.164
	Gain Relative to S&P 500 Index*	142 bps	−148 bps	0.132	−0.149
Large Cap	**Wisdom Tree LargeCap Dividend Index**	**11.28%**	**13.25%**	**0.479**	**0.851**
	S&P 500 Index*	10.46%	14.76%	0.392	1.000
	Gain Relative to S&P 500 Index	83 bps	−151 bps	0.088	−0.149
Mid Cap	**Wisdom Tree MidCap Dividend Index**	**14.09%**	**15.04%**	**0.635**	**0.866**
	Hypothetical Reference Index—Mid Cap	12.82%	17.54%	0.488	1.078
	Gain Relative to Hypothetical Reference Index	127 bps	−250 bps	0.147	−0.213
Small Cap	**Wisdom Tree SmallCap Dividend Index**	**15.71%**	**16.06%**	**0.737**	**0.847**
	Hypothetical Reference Index—Small Cap	13.38%	20.96%	0.485	1.157
	Gain Relative to Hypothetical Reference Index	233 bps	−490 bps	0.251	−0.310

40

As you can see, dividend weighting instead of capitalization weighting produced returns that were meaningfully ahead of the capitalization-weighted indexes with less volatility.

❑   ❑   ❑

THE GREENBLATT MODEL

This next tool was developed by hedge fund manager Joel Greenblatt. Like Cripps and Siegel, Greenblatt had a theory. It was a very simple but very logical theory.

Greenblatt theorized that the best stocks should be from companies with two attributes: very high earnings relative to stock price and the ability to reinvest a dollar of earnings back into the company at a very high rate of return.

He believed that the stocks with the highest earnings yields offered the greatest value. If one stock were selling for $20 per share and earning $4 per share, he was getting a 20 percent earnings yield, and all other things being equal, this was a better investment than a company that had an earnings yield of just 10 percent.

Of equal importance was what the company did with the earnings. Greenblatt reasoned that companies that could reinvest their earnings back into the company and grow the money at high rates of return (return on working capital) had to be better stocks than those that had to reinvest at more modest rates of return.

He created a simple SPM that used just these two variables, the companies' earnings yield and its return on working capital, and dubbed it the "Magic Formula."

First, he sorted his portfolio based on earnings yield, assigning a value of one to the company with the highest earnings yield, a value of two to the company with the second highest earnings yield, and so on. Then he similarly ranked the companies based on return on working capital.

In this way the companies earning the most on each dollar of retained earnings were identified. Greenblatt then summed the rankings and selected the stocks with the lowest scores. These were companies with very high earnings, able to earn high returns on retained earnings.

The results, published in his book, are on the following pages.

GREENBLATT SPM 1988–2004 3500 LARGEST U.S. STOCKS

	Greenblatt SPM	Market Average*	S&P 500
1988	27.1%	24.8%	16.6%
1989	44.6	18.0	31.7
1990	1.7	(16.1)	(3.1)
1991	70.6	45.6	30.5
1992	32.4	11.4	7.6
1993	17.2	15.9	10.1
1994	22.0	(4.5)	1.3
1995	34.0	29.1	37.6
1996	173	14.9	23.0
1997	40.4	16.8	33.4
1998	25.5	(2.0)	28.6
1999	53.0	36.1	21.0
2000	7.9	(16.8)	(9.1)
2001	69.8	11.5	(11.9)
2002	(4.0)	(24.2)	(22.1)
2003	79.9	68.8	28.7
2004	19.3	17.8	10.9
	30.8%	12.3%	12.4%

*Note: The "market average" return is an equally weighted average of our 1,000-stock universe. The S&P 500 index is a market-weighted index of 500 large stocks.

41

Greenblatt then applied his methodology to the one thousand largest publicly traded stocks. While the results were less dramatic, they were still impressive.

GREENBLATT SPM 1988–2004 1000 LARGEST U.S. STOCKS

	Greenblatt SPM	Market Average*	S&P 500
1988	29.4%	19.6%	16.6%
1989	30.0	27.6	31.7
1990	(6.0)	(7.1)	(3.1)
1991	51.5	34.4	30.5
1992	16.4	10.3	7.6
1993	0.5	14.4	10.1
1994	15.3	0.5	1.3
1995	55.9	31.4	37.6
1996	37.4	16.2	23.0
1997	41.0	19.6	33.4
1998	32.6	9.9	28.6
1999	14.4	35.1	21.0
2000	12.8	(14.5)	(9.1)
2001	38.2	(9.2)	(11.9)
2002	(25.3)	(22.7)	(22.1)
2003	50.5	41.4	28.7
2004	27.6	17.3	10.9
	22.9%	11.7%	12.4%

*Note: The "market average" return is an equally weighted average of our 1,000-stock universe. The S&P 500 index is a market-weighted index of 500 large stocks.

42

Finally, Greenblatt applied his methodology to the twenty-five hundred largest publicly traded stocks. He divided them into deciles with the top 10 percent of the highest-scoring stocks in the first decile.

STUDY OF 2500 LARGEST COMPANIES GROUPED BY GREENBLATT SPM

Annualized Return (1988–2004)	
Group 1 (Highest Score)	17.9%
Group 2	15.6
Group 3	14.8
Group 4	14.2
Group 5	14.1
Group 6	12.7
Group 7	11.3
Group 8	10.1
Group 9	5.2
Group 10 (Lowest Score)	2.5

43

As the chart shows, there was a strong correlation between a group's score and its performance. Indeed, Greenblatt's formula is extremely logical, extremely simple, and extremely effective.

❑   ❑   ❑

TINY TITANS

The final SPM we will discuss was developed by James O'Shaughnessy, a fund manager with a very uncommon approach to investing; he selects his securities entirely by using SPMs.

He has written a number of books, including *What Works on Wall Street*, in which he makes the case for using statistics exclusively for selecting securities. O'Shaughnessy discusses a number of models in his book, but there is one model that has produced robust returns almost impossible for a mutual fund to replicate. This is because the strategy involves investing in microcap companies.

O'Shaughnessy reasoned that stocks of the smallest companies were the ones most likely to be significantly mispriced.

This is because microcap stocks are, for the most part, uninvestable due to their small size and limited float (the amount of shares that trade every day).

If he could identify small companies selling at low valuation ratios but moving up in price very rapidly, he could find companies that would make great investments.

O'Shaughnessy developed a model based on this category of companies, which he called the Tiny Titans. With this SPM, he screened for stocks with market capitalizations between $25 million and $250 million and price-to-sales ratios below one. He used these screens to develop a list of small companies with low price-to-sales ratios and with great sales leverage.[44] Sales leverage is important because for many companies, it is much easier to increase profit margins through cost cutting and eliminating discounts than it is to increase sales.

Many stocks with low price-to-sales ratios, however, are in commodity businesses with permanently low margins. Grocery stores are a good example. While many have very low price-to-sales ratios, not all grocery stores are good stocks. Grocery stores historically have had very small profit margins because they are a commodity business; it is very difficult for them to exploit their sales leverage. Because people consume groceries every day, they are very price sensitive. So a grocery that tried to institute an 8 percent price hike would probably expect to see its sales drop meaningfully.

To avoid selecting stocks such as these, O'Shaughnessy's next rule was to purchase the twenty-five stocks with the highest price appreciation over the past twelve months. This way, he was selecting companies that were relatively cheap (based on their sales numbers), underfollowed by Wall Street (based on their size), and doing something very exciting (based on their stock price). These were companies that could also capitalize on their sales leverage. They could increase their prices by offering a service with high perceived value but at a relatively small cost to the company. In this case almost all of the price increase will fall to the company's bottom line, enhancing earnings.

Verbatim corporation is a good example of a company that capitalized on its sales leverage. In the fall of 1979, 5.25-inch floppy disks were a new technology, and Verbatim had approximately one-third of the market share. But the company had a reputation for poor disk quality, due to flaws in the manufacturing process. Costs mounted as the company replaced faulty disks and worked to reengineer the disk design. Meanwhile, earnings and stock price both plummeted.

In response, the company instituted a program of testing each and every disk, and while this was an expensive process, it worked. Eventually, customers were convinced they had the best disks on the market, and confidence in the company returned. Sales started to increase. Over the next two years, the stock price increased more than tenfold.[45]

So how did O'Shaughnessy's Tiny Titans do? Take a look at the following chart:

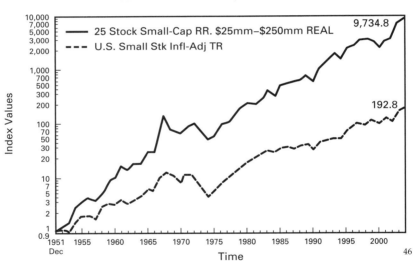

TINY TITANS SPM
TERMINAL VALUE OF $1 INVESTED IN 1951

According to O'Shaughnessy, the Tiny Titans (top line) averaged 18.92 percent per year over the course of fifty-three years. One thousand dollars invested in these stocks in 1951 grew to more than $9,700,000 in 2004.

O'Shaughnessy is careful to point out that even though the Tiny Titans had an extraordinary record, the returns were extremely volatile. The standard deviation of the returns was a stomach-churning 39 percent. Statistics tell us that about two-thirds of our observations will fall within one standard deviation of the mean. That means that one-third of the time, the returns of this portfolio will be either greater than 58 percent or less than negative 20 percent. This is a huge disparity. This strategy is extremely volatile, which means that a rough period can be very rough indeed.

The obvious difficulty with this type of strategy is the behavioral risk that you will give up on it after a period of poor performance. Perhaps the best way to implement a strategy such as this is to start with a relatively small amount of money and faithfully add to it.

12

INCORPORATING **SPM**S INTO **Y**OUR **I**NVESTMENT **S**TRATEGY

A s I said earlier in the book, SPMs should be used as part of an overall financial plan. Individuals not highly savvy about financial planning should work with an appropriately credentialed financial advisor to help them develop and implement a personalized plan to meet their financial needs.

With this in mind, let's look at how some theoretical individuals might incorporate SPMs as part of their overall plans. Keep in mind that these examples are for illustrative purposes only and do not constitute recommendations of these strategies.

❏   ❏   ❏

First, let's meet Hannah Bird. Hannah is thirty-five and has her own interior decorating practice. She has about $110,000 in investments, including a Roth IRA with $28,000 and some stock in AT&T, which she inherited from her grandmother. She also has a technology fund with $11,000 (bought on the recommendation of an old boyfriend), and five other stocks.

Hannah is goal oriented and organized in her business. But she realizes that, in contrast, there is no synergy among her investments; her assets do not work together in a coordinated way. She decides to make an appointment with Abigail Scarfy, an investment advisor who specializes in using SPMs.

With Abigail's help, Hannah takes several steps:

- She decides to place her Roth IRA into an all-cap portfolio through a fee-based account using clearly defined rules that govern when and how stocks are bought or sold for her portfolio.

- She then uses the balance of her assets to construct a portfolio of twenty-five stocks using a microcapitalization portfolio selected by statistical prediction. Hannah plans to keep her winners until they have turned into long-term gains and to sell her losers after six months if they no longer meet the selection criteria. Again, clearly defined rules govern when stocks are added or eliminated from her portfolio.

- Hannah also decides to add $5,000 per year to her Roth account and to start a SEP retirement account for her business.

With these few changes, she now feels she has a plan to follow and, more important, there is a synergistic relationship among her investments. Also, of utmost importance, she feels she has an advisor who can keep her on track.

Meet Louis and Betty Johnson. Louis is fifty-eight and Betty is fifty-five. They have been married thirty-five years and have three grown children. Louis just retired from the power company, where he worked as a lineman. Betty has been a homemaker.

Louis plans to begin collecting Social Security payments when he is sixty-two. The Johnsons have $200,000 in power company stock, $40,000 in a credit union, and a $400,000 401(k) rollover in a stock mutual fund. They need about $40,000 a year to cover the gap until Louis receives his company pension and Social Security in four years.

The Johnsons have been pleased with the growth stock fund they chose within the company 401(k) but are thinking now of investing more for income instead of growth.

At the company's preretirement seminar, they learned they can take early Pre-Age 59½ rule 72(t) distributions and avoid a penalty if they choose to withdraw funds from their 401(k) earlier than age 59½.

Their nephew, who recently began his career at a small financial planning firm that sells mutual funds and insurance, has recommended they do an IRA rollover and invest all $400,000 in a high-yield bond fund that pays 8 percent. Louis estimates that with the 8 percent from the bond fund, he will earn $32,000 per year and, adding in $8,000 per year he receives in dividends from his company stock, he should have enough income until he reaches age sixty-two.

What Louis has failed to realize, however, is that this strategy is extremely risky.

With his pension and his savings, Louis and Betty are indeed in a position to enjoy a comfortable retirement, but there is not much room for error with this plan.

First, he has more than 30 percent of his liquid assets invested in his company stock. This is never a good idea no matter how good the company.

Second, placing their entire 401(k) in a high-yield bond fund exposes them to credit risk and interest rate risk.

Let's look at how they can instead integrate SPMs into their planning to reduce risk and enhance their overall return.

- First, Louis and Betty should consider a self-liquidating fixed-income portfolio, funded by the power company stock. By selling $150,000 worth of stock, they can create enough cash to meet their needs until their pension begins.

- They should then invest this cash into laddered certificates of deposit that mature over the next four years to meet their income needs. (When selling the stock, they should be careful to ask their broker to mark the order ticket shares by highest cost to reduce the tax consequence of their sale.)

- Louis and Betty decide to retain their $40,000 credit union account as a liquidity fund to finance any unexpected emergencies.

- They purchase long-term care policies and now feel they can invest the money in their 401(k) to maximize their long-term returns.

- To ensure some international exposure, they place $100,000 into an international mutual fund.

- They place $240,000 of their portfolio into an all-cap portfolio constructed on a value-based SPM and place $60,000 into an aggressive small-cap portfolio. Again, clearly defined rules govern changes in the portfolio going forward.

While some advisors would recommend the Johnsons put a considerable amount into bonds, Louis and Betty realize they have a fixed annuity from his employer that will pay them for the rest of their lives, once Louis reaches age sixty-two.

An annuity is simply fixed income. People who have fixed annuities (provided by their employers or insurance companies) that provide them enough money to meet their living expenses can invest a higher percentage of their dollars in the stock market, versus those who must rely on their investment returns for living expenses.

Both the small-cap and all-cap portfolios are diversified among all sectors of the market. These two SPMs together provide exposure to large-, mid-, and small-cap stocks. The mutual fund gives exposure to international markets, and the fixed annuity is the bond component. The Johnsons are well positioned for the future.

❑   ❑   ❑

Let's meet Robert and Susan Goodson. Robert is fifty-six and Susan is forty-two, and it is a second marriage for both. They have one child together, Elizabeth, age three. Robert has twin boys from his first marriage, age eleven. Susan has no children from her first marriage.

Robert recently sold his manufacturing business. After taxes he netted $1.6 million. He has $950,000 to roll over from the company pension plan. He will also receive $200,000 for the next ten years as payment for the business. Susan earns $60,000 per year as the executive director of a local charity.

Robert admits he has spent way too much time in the past managing his investments. He has tried day trading and mutual fund switching strategies without success. He was leaning toward investing in index funds until his CPA told him he should consider meeting with an advisor who could help him implement a strategy using SPMs.

After considering his situation, Robert realizes that he does not need to invest aggressively to live comfortably. His most important goal is to protect what he has. Nevertheless, his financial position allows him to take some risks.

With this in mind, and with his advisor's help, Robert makes the following changes to his plan:

- He places half of his cash on hand, $800,000, into a laddered municipal bond strategy.

- He takes the other $800,000 cash and invests it into the forty largest stocks in the S&P 500 (based on capitalization).

- His advisor creates a custom portfolio, within Robert's IRA, weighted the same as the S&P 500, minus its forty largest stocks, using a statistical prediction model based on the companies' price-to-sales ratios.

- With the cash flow from the municipal bonds and the stock portfolio, he sets up a microcapitalization portfolio designed to take advantage of pricing inefficiencies in illiquid companies.

Let's compare the consequences of Robert's new strategy versus his earlier plan to purchase index funds.

Because Robert's portfolio is weighted by capitalization and sector to the S&P and because he owns the forty largest stocks in the S&P 500, he has substantially reduced his risk of trailing the S&P 500. Furthermore, by using SPMs, he has given himself the opportunity to beat the index.

In addition, Robert has preserved some very important options for reducing his taxes that he would not have had with an index fund.

For example, let's say that the large-cap stock portfolio Robert purchased has appreciated 30 percent, but some stocks are up much more than 30 percent. Assume the most highly appreciated stock in their portfolio has doubled. The Goodsons can give shares of that stock to charity, thus avoiding capital gains. They can then use the cash from dividends and interest and purchase new shares to keep their portfolio in balance. The new shares will have a higher cost basis than the donated shares, reducing future tax liability.

He will also be able to cherry-pick his losses from the stock portfolio by selling his depreciated stocks. Again, assuming his large-cap portfolio is up 30 percent, he still might have some losing stocks. He can sell the stocks that are down, generate a loss to offset other capital gains and some income, and reduce his taxes. When his boys are ready for college, he has the option to gift them appreciated stock and let them sell the shares to pay their tuitions, thus taking advantage of the boys' lower tax rates.

While I realize that all of the tax planning above could in some circumstances be accomplished with an index fund, it would be accomplished much less efficiently. With an index fund, you can donate appreciated shares to charity and sell depreciated shares to take a loss, but in all cases, you are working with the cost of the fund shares. But the underlying stocks make the most extreme moves and give the best opportunity for tax-motivated transactions. With an index fund, these opportunities are simply averaged away, resulting in less tax savings.

More important, many index funds available today have huge embedded gains. If the public's love affair with these funds ever wanes and there are meaningful liquidations, index fund investors could face large unexpected tax liabilities. This is because, with large-scale liquidations, the fund company would be forced to sell highly appreciated securities, and by law these gains would have to be distributed to shareholders as capital gain distributions.

While index funds do have a place for small investors, affluent investors clearly have much better options by including SPMs.

PART IV
Embracing Nakedness

INTRODUCTION:
EXPOSING THE INDUSTRY

T he mutual fund industry charges investors hundreds of millions of dollars each year to provide fund perfor-mance that is generally worse than the market averages. The following chart, reprinted from *What Works on Wall Street* by James O'Shaughnessy, shows the percentage of funds that have beaten the S&P 500 for the preceding ten years. As you can see, the overwhelming majority of funds underperform the market index. Over any given ten-year period, on average, less than one fund in four will beat the S&P 500.

PERCENT OF ALL EQUITY FUNDS WITH 10-YEAR TRACK RECRDS
BEATING THE S&P 500. PERIODS ENDING DECEMBER 31 IN EACH YEAR.

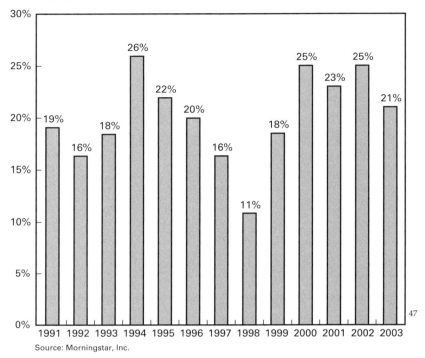

Source: Morningstar, Inc.

With trillions of dollars at stake, why don't mutual funds, which spend hundreds of millions of dollars on research each year, do better? We know that part of the reason is that many reject actuarial strategies and, as a result, make judgment errors that hurt their performance. Moreover, there are structural problems with the fund industry that act as a further handicap.

There is a myth, propagated by the mutual fund industry, that investment advisors serve clients better by recommending they place money with fund companies, rather than helping these individuals manage it themselves.

Mutual fund companies often point out that they have offices all over the world and employ hundreds of analysts and make thousands of visits to companies. The question is then, "How can an individual financial advisor compete with the massive firepower of a mutual fund giant?"

Maybe we all need some history lessons.

13

MILITARY HISTORY AND PORTFOLIO MANAGEMENT

I would like to take you back to a class I took at the United States Military Academy back in 1982 called History of the Military Art.

Of all the classes I took at West Point, no class is more memorable. I remember this class especially for the instructor, Captain Layman. He was definitely a martinet. You did not dare walk into that class without your shoes shined and your reading assignment completed. While at first we all feared him, by the end of the class, we all loved him. Captain Layman was such a great instructor because he showed us how to apply the lessons of history to gain insight into our daily lives and human behavior in general.

The Vietnam War gave Captain Layman fertile ground to teach us about history and life. There are some very important lessons from this conflict that apply to other fields, including portfolio management.

If you look at the globe and look at Vietnam and compare it to the United States, you can see that the United States is vastly larger. If you compare the GNP of the United States to the GNP of Vietnam, the difference is even more dramatic than the difference in land mass.

So why did the United States lose this war? How was a tiny country able to frustrate the strategic objectives of the most powerful nation in the world? There are many reasons for this, but I want to focus on just two.

The first lesson from Vietnam is that there are **constraints to power and resources** that can interfere with the accomplishment of the objective. This goes against those who assert that the United States could have ended the war victoriously anytime by using its nuclear weapons. The truth, though, is that while we had nuclear capability, there were political, economic, and social constraints that prevented the United States from using nuclear power.

Now compare these to the constraints placed on a fund manager. Like the United States in Vietnam, mutual fund managers have many self-imposed restrictions that prevent them from bringing the full weight of their judgment on the portfolio. While the regulatory bodies place a number of constraints on fund managers, many fund companies place even more restrictive constraints on their funds.

For example, a large-cap growth fund must buy large-cap growth stocks if that is what its prospectus mandates. This is true even if the manager believes the best values in the market at certain times are small-cap growth stocks. A technology fund buys only technology stocks if that is what the prospectus mandates, regardless of whether they represent good values at all times.

There is nothing inherently wrong with any of these approaches, but remember, the decision of an investment company to offer a fund that restricts its stock purchases to a particular segment of the market is frequently a decision made by the marketing department, not the investment committee.

When the technology boom started in the 1990s, many fund companies rushed out new technology funds. In the eighties, when mortgage rates reached double digits, fund companies rolled out government mortgage funds. Fund companies often provide what investors want, not what they need.

The key difference between investing based on a well-constructed SPM and investing based on the rules in the mutual fund prospectus is that the SPM rules are created to maximize return.

The business end of the mutual fund industry frequently creates funds the company thinks will sell well. Sometimes the rules in the prospectus are designed to distinguish that particular fund from other company offerings and allow the fund company to increase its market share.

Besides regulatory and self-imposed constraints, another factor that limits fund managers' ability is the size of their portfolios. The larger the fund, the fewer stocks available from which to choose. This is because a stock's float (the number of shares that trade each day) is limited. If a company trades around $25 per share and trades 200,000 shares on an average day, about $5,000,000 worth of that stock changes hands that day.

A relatively small fund with $250 million in assets that wanted to get a 2 percent position (i.e., 2 percent of their holdings) in that stock would need to buy about 200,000 shares. They might be able to accomplish this in a few days without moving the price too much.

But a $10 billion dollar fund that wanted to get a 2 percent position in this company would need forty times as much stock as the smaller fund, or 8 million shares. They would have to buy 200,000 shares a day for about two months to get their position. This is virtually impossible to do without moving up the stock price significantly. And when they wanted to sell, they would have the problem of liquidating the position without driving the stock price way down.

As an example, Peter Lynch in *One Up on Wall Street* lamented that the sheer size of his Magellan fund, $9 billion, was the biggest handicap he had. It reminds me of Napoleon's army, which, at the size of about 60,000 men, was a highly maneuverable, extremely successful, elite force in the Austrian and Italian campaigns. But when the force grew tenfold and Napoleon sent 600,000 men into Russia, he lost his ability to maneuver and was routed.

Another lesson from the Vietnam War is that massive resources will not always be enough to accomplish an objective. The important lesson? **Fight on your own terms.**

During the Vietnam War, we fought the North Vietnamese regular army, which fought like any other army. But we also fought the Viet Cong, which was made up of citizen soldiers. They were farmers by day, but at night they became guerillas who attacked our forces. They were very difficult to defeat because they were able to melt into the landscape.

The Viet Cong were especially effective because of their tactics. For example, when they ambushed a U.S. convoy, they would strike with surprise and tremendous ferocity. Then after a brief period, the attack would abruptly stop, and the Viet Cong forces would slip away, keenly aware of how long it would take before the U.S. Army's helicopter gunships arrived.

The Viet Cong's strategy was to avoid battles in locations where the U.S. Army could demonstrate its superiority. In other words, they found a way to fight on their own terms, when they had the advantage. Ultimately, these tactics allowed the North Vietnamese to prevail against the United States.

Thinking about the Viet Cong's military tactics can help an individual investor understand how to select a successful strategy.

If you try to pick stocks the same way a mutual fund portfolio manager does, it's very unlikely you will be able to beat him. What you need are different tactics, optimized for your situation.

SPMs are ideally suited for individual investors because they provide opportunities for individuals that are not available to mutual funds and large institutional managers. For example, some SPMs rely on buying stocks that are difficult for large mutual funds to purchase, while other SPMs implement trading strategies that are difficult to use with large amounts of money.

14

Recent History: Lessons from the 2008 Meltdown

The first draft of *The Naked Portfolio Manager* was written over a nine-month period beginning in November of 2007. When I began writing the book, I had no idea that 2008 would be such a terrible year to be an investor.

With the S&P 500 losing 37 percent of its value, it was one of the worst years ever for the index. But smaller company stocks lost money too. The Russell 2000 small stock growth index dropped 38.5 percent, and the Russell Mid Cap Value Index dropped 38.4 percent. Overseas stocks were no place to hide either. The Japanese market dropped 29.1 percent, and Pacific markets (without Japan) dropped a stunning 50 percent. European markets also dropped precipitously. The UK market dropped 48.3 percent, and Europe (without the UK) fared nearly as badly, dropping 45 percent.

Fixed income markets suffered also. The high-yield index dropped 26.2 percent, and emerging debt lost 14.7 percent. Even municipal bond securities, a stalwart investment of conservative investors, had a negative return of 2.5 percent.[48]

The year 2008 was truly an awful year for investors. If you started to think about abandoning traditional methods of equity investing, 2008 provided a plethora of reasons to do so.

One of the most important stories of 2008 was the indictment of Bernard Madoff, a former chairman of NASDAQ, on charges that his investment company defrauded thousands of investors of billions of dollars in an illegal Ponzi scheme.

As of this writing (January of 2009), Madoff has been convicted of nothing, and people are, of course, innocent until proven guilty. But what is clear is that thousands of people lost money investing in a black box strategy—a veritable Pandora's black box.

Investopedia says that in a black box model, "the system contains formulas and calculations that the user does not see nor need to know to use the system." Many people believed that Madoff had developed a proprietary trading system that allowed him to provide consistently superior returns.

When asked by a *Barron's* reporter in 2001 how his system worked, he responded, "It's no one's business what goes on here…. It's a proprietary strategy. I can't go into it in great detail."[49]

Naked SPM strategies—completely transparent—avoid many of the risks associated with the secret black box systems such as the one Madoff used. Investors know exactly how their money is invested.

The Madoff fiasco also illustrates that confirmation bias continues to plague investors.

Madoff was marketed as a brilliant man with a highly sophisticated strategy that was too complicated for most people to understand. Investors wanted to believe they were among a select group who had been fortunate enough to be invited to invest with a man with the Midas touch, who could consistently produce outstanding investment returns.

Indeed, according to the *Nightly Business Report*, clients included such well-heeled investors as Norman Braman (former owner of the Philadelphia Eagles), Senator Frank Lautenberg (D-NJ), Steven Spielberg's charitable foundations, J. Ezra Merkin (chairman of GMAC Financial Services), and many other wealthy individuals and foundations.[50]

It appears that these very sophisticated investors never asked themselves, "What could be wrong with this investment approach?" If they had done any investigation at all, they would easily have found reasons to be alarmed. For instance, *Barron's* first ran an article in 2001 saying that Madoff was running a front for his favored investors.[51] Other people, including fellow hedge fund manager Harry Markopoulos, were saying six years ago that the Madoff fund was a Ponzi scheme.[52]

Yet these seemingly savvy investors were seduced by the idea that they had found a truly brilliant man who was going to make lots of money for them on a consistent basis with very little risk, and they overlooked ideas contrary to what they preferred to believe.

❑　　❑　　❑

The next lesson from 2008 is a painfully obvious one: you cannot count on fund managers to protect you in bear markets. On the Morningstar Web site, Russel Kinnel wrote:

> No matter how you slice it, fund investors and managers alike suffered a setback in 2008 ... just about everyone lost money—and not just a little, but staggering amounts. The average fund lost more than 30% in 2008.

Then Morningstar proceeded to give the award of fund manager of the year to Charlie Dreifus of the Royce Special Equity Fund, which lost only 19.5 percent. Dreifus deserves much credit for turning in a very respectable return in such an awful market, but with thousands of mutual funds, what does it say for the fund industry when Morningstar selects a fund that lost nearly a fifth of its value?

It makes me think about the University of Texas Medical School interviews of its eight hundred applicants for medical school, discussed in chapter 3. After spending thousands of man-hours and who knows how much money trying to predict the best candidates, the collective wisdom of the school admissions officers was no better than a simple, inexpensive SPM based on class rank and GRE score.

Similarly, if a fund that lost nearly a fifth of its value is the best the fund industry has to offer, wouldn't it make more sense to save the fees you pay to own mutual funds and invest using SPMs?

❑　　❑　　❑

So how did the strategies that we discussed in the book fare during the 2008 meltdown?

According to www.wisdomtree.com, the WisdomTree Large Cap Dividend Fund—a fund managed exclusively by an SPM designed to correspond closely to the Large Cap Dividend Index—returned −35.86 percent for the year, slightly more than one percent better than the S&P 500. This return is consistent with the long-term average excess return of 83 basis points that Siegel found in his white paper (discussed in chapter 11).

While 1 percent may not seem like very much, remember that over a lifetime of investing, increasing your average returns by just one percent per year will allow you to accumulate substantially more wealth.

The **redline strategy** fared slightly worse than the S&P 500 in 2008. All redline low stocks without dividends returned −39.1 percent versus a return of −38.5 percent for the S&P 500 exclusive of dividends. Comparing the returns of the all redline low stocks to the S&P 500 exclusive of dividends for the past six years is interesting. See the chart on the following page.

ANNUALIZED RETURN OF
REDLINE LOW STOCKS VERSUS S&P 500
2003–2008

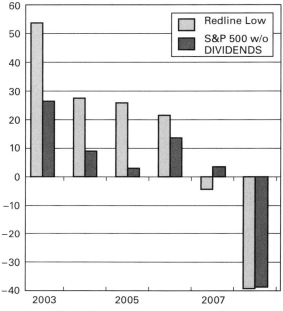

Source: The Stifel Nicolaus Equity Compass Strategy Group.

As you can see, the redline strategy has handily beat the S&P 500 over the past six years. The fact that the strategy trailed slightly in 2007 was certainly not a reason to abandon the strategy. Why did some investors using this strategy give up and go to cash in 2008? They underestimated their ability to ride through a difficult market.

The fact is the market is volatile, and this SPM is designed to guide investors into mispriced stocks, not to get them out of the market when it goes through severe corrections.

❏   ❏   ❏

On a conference call conducted on January 7, 2009, Richard Cripps, Chief Investment Officer of a regional brokerage firm, made an interesting point: during the past two bear markets, strategic asset allocation (also known as modern portfolio theory) failed to mitigate large losses.

Investors have been coached for years to diversify among asset classes by investing their portfolios in a mix of asset classes. These might include large-capitalization stocks, small-capitalization stocks, international stocks, and high-yield bonds, for example. The idea was that if one part of the market did poorly, the other parts might do much better and improve your overall results. Of course, in 2008 the decline was so broad that many investors with broadly diversified asset allocation suffered large losses.

Cripps suggested that SPMs might offer an interesting alternative to traditional asset allocation as a means of protecting investors' capital.

He pointed out that the return of an equity portfolio was influenced by both the individual securities selected as well as the overall market. He theorized that an algorithm could be constructed that reduced the equity exposure in a downward market. However, Cripps also noted that such an algorithm might also reduce the portfolio's return in upward markets.

But the idea that investors might eschew traditional asset allocation in favor of an SPM-based methodology to reduce risk is certainly one that deserves further investigation.

At the time of this writing, Joel Greenblatt had not published updated returns through 2008 for **the Greenblatt SPM** and James O'Shaughnessy had not yet updated the returns of the **Tiny Titans** portfolio. However, the Web site www.whatworksonwallstreet .com had an interesting comment that O'Shaughnessy made on July 29, 1999, after a portfolio he managed had rebounded sharply after a long period of lackluster performance. I think the comment is as applicable today as it was then:

> If you're honest with yourself, you'll see the folly of trying to out guess the market. You'll see it's a fool's game to try to move from fund to fund based on what's hot at the moment. You'll realize that over the short-term anything can happen, and that to extrapolate the short-term into the future leads you down many blind alleys.

You can also see from these examples that over the longer term, Strategy Indexing [O'Shaughnessy's term for SPMs] *has worked*—sometimes when you're just about to give up hope. Our constant challenge is to keep the faith. But think how happy we'll be when we need our savings. Patience and long-term focus will pay off, and we remain convinced that Strategy Indexing will be the revenge of the patient investor.

I could not have said it better.

❏   ❏   ❏

There are important lessons to be drawn from the examples in this chapter: it is essential not just to select good SPMs, but also to employ behavioral strategies to help you stay with your investment strategy through difficult times. For many people, it is extremely important to work with someone who will help you stay the course as abandoning strategies at the wrong time can prevent you from participating in the recovery.

Finally, remember that scores of studies have concluded that human experts would get better results using their expertise to *construct models* for the purpose of making predictions, instead of *making the predictions themselves.*

The year 2008 again saw investors disappointed in the abilities of both judgment-based portfolio managers and black box strategists. Consistently applying SPMs in a disciplined manner, while not an investing panacea, reduces the risks associated with human judgment and black box myopia and gives investors an edge in their decision making.

15

CONCLUSION

In this book I have tried to make the case that decisions regarding stock selection are best made using statistical models and that even the best traditional portfolio managers could improve their results by creating their own rules-based decision algorithm and sticking to those rules.

In building my case, I have used very few statistics, instead relying on anecdotes, analogies, and drawings, which are better suited for my purposes. I find that these tools exemplify concepts and make them easier for people to remember and implement.

James O'Shaughnessy's excellent book *What Works on Wall Street* makes the case for SPMs by using reams of statistics. In the book he identifies dozens of actuarial strategies that produced market-beating results. While his book is extremely well researched, it is filled with statistical charts, which is not to everyone's liking. Nevertheless, I highly recommend it for those who need more statistical proof of the ideas expressed in this book.

Both the statistics compiled by O'Shaughnessy and the arguments in this book support a fundamental truth that very few Wall Street professionals understand: what we have learned about human judges in other disciplines applies to human judges (portfolio managers) in the stock market.

Now that you've read this book, if you ignore the Wall Street noise and consistently invest based on statistical prediction, you will be better prepared to avoid the bad stock market odds that accompany many financial products and invest with a meaningful edge enjoyed by very few investors.

Thank you for reading *The Naked Portfolio Manager*. I hope you enjoyed reading it as much as I enjoyed writing it. I am sure there will be a *Naked Portfolio Manager Two*.

I can't really say the book is finished, though; it truly is a work in progress. As I wrote it, I was constantly finding new data, new examples, and new statistical models that supported its premise. You will find this information and more at my Web site: www.NakedPortfolioManager.com. I look forward to hearing from you.

The views expressed herein are those of the author and do not represent the views of the broker-dealer by whom he is employed, its officers, or its other employees.

About the Author

Bob Fischer brings a rare combination of skills, talents, and background to his career as senior portfolio manager and advisor for affluent individuals at a national brokerage firm. His noteworthy success in the investment field is based upon his in-depth knowledge of decision making, which he applies in a disciplined, rules-based approach: the application of Statistical Prediction Methods.

A student of human behavior since childhood, Bob studied the games of world-class chess masters to learn how their decision-making processes led them to victory. At least in part as a result of his studies, he was awarded the title of life master by the United States Chess Federation. He attended the U.S. Military Academy at West Point and pursued a military career in which he studied classical military decision making and problem solving. After serving the nation as a military officer, he began a career as an investment advisor with a regional brokerage firm. It was there that he again observed that people's decision-making processes—this time regarding investments—were frequently flawed. He saw firsthand how emotions often got the best of clients and caused them to make suboptimal decisions. This led him to develop new techniques for helping clients improve their decision making and realize better long-term investment results.

Bob has written numerous articles on investment and financial planning for industry publications including *Financial Planning, Registered Representative, Personal Investing, The American Association of Individual Investors Journal, On Wall Street*, and *Disclosures Magazine* (the publication of the Virginia CPA Society). He lives with his family in Midlothian, Virginia.

Glossary

Algorithm – A clearly defined, step-by-step serial process used to come to a decision.

Black Box Method – A method of investing in which the investor does not need to know or understand (and is often not allowed to know) the data input or how the data is processed to use the outcome.

Clinical decision making – A decision-making approach in which an expert or professional relying on his training, experience, and judgment determines the course of action.

Configural thinking – A method of thinking that requires the decision maker to consider the entire problem at once. It contrasts with serial thinking in which a problem is solved in steps.

Confirmation bias – This is a thinking deficiency in which the decision maker searches for ideas that support his initial impression and ignores or dismisses evidence that is contrary to his preconceived idea.

Correlation – A statistical technique that shows how strongly two variables are related. The *correlation coefficient* is a number between negative one and positive one that explains how well two variables are related. Positive one means that the two variables are perfectly correlated, and negative one means they are inversely correlated. A correlation coefficient of zero means that there is no relationship between the variables.

Disconfirmation strategy – A thinking approach in which the decision maker actively seeks reasons the initial impression may be incorrect. Disconfirmation strategies frequently lead to new insights otherwise difficult to uncover.

Efficient market hypothesis – A theory that holds that over the long run, investors should not expect to outperform the market averages because all relevant information about equities is known and priced in the market.

Equity position – Owners of shares of stock are said to have an equity position in the company. This differs from bond holders who have loaned the company money in anticipation of receiving bond interest payments.

Evidence-based medicine – This approach encourages the practitioner to use knowledge gained from the application of the scientific method in controlled studies. EBM, however, recognizes that there are many medical decisions that involve value and quality of life that are only partially subject to the scientific method. EBM seeks to segregate those parts of the medical practice that are subject to the scientific method in order to select treatments with the best expected benefit for the patient.

Hedge fund – A mutual fund that is formed as a limited partnership that in some cases uses high-risk strategies in an attempt to produce large profits.

Heuristics – Mental shortcuts that we use to simplify our decision making. These shortcuts save us tremendous amounts of time and energy. For example, when crossing the street, if we see an oncoming car very near and moving very fast, we wait. If it is far away and moving very slowly, we cross the street. There is no need to do any time-distance math calculation since our simple rule of thumb (when to cross versus not cross the street) serves us well. Heuristics can get us in trouble, however, when we use mental shortcuts to make decisions that should be made with analysis.

Independent outcomes – Two outcomes are said to be independent if the result of one does not affect the other. For example, the number that comes up on a roulette wheel would be independent of the sum of the dice at the craps table.

Index – A group of stocks selected to represent a particular market segment.

Managed account – This is an investment account owned by an individual investor and managed by a professional money manager. It differs from a mutual fund where investors own a share of a pooled fund. With a managed account, an investor owns the actual securities in the account and is not part of a pool.

Market timing – This refers to short-term trading of securities in an attempt to capitalize on minor moves in the market.

Meta-analysis – The statistical synthesis of data from a group of similar studies to produce a pooled result.

Naked strategies – These are *simple*, rules-based methods of coming to a decision. While the construction of the rules may be extremely complicated, the application of the rules is relatively simple. Naked strategies are characterized by relatively few rules and a small number of variables. Unlike black box strategies, naked strategies are always transparent. That is, there is nothing hidden from investors.

Narrative fallacy – This is a confirmation bias thinking error in which the thinker creates a story to explain a fortuitous event. Normally the story reflects very positively on the thinker. For example, a gambler who takes a rabbit's foot to the casino and wins may attribute the win to the luck of the rabbit's foot without considering that other gamblers may take a rabbit's foot with them and not win.

Rule of large numbers – This mathematical principle holds that if a large sample is drawn from a population, the sample is likely to be similar to the population. Conversely, a smaller sample drawn from the same sample is less likely to have properties similar to the group. The corollary of short time periods tells us that when we invest for short time periods, we are much less likely to earn the long-term average of the asset class we are investing in than if we invested for a longer time period. Investors often fail to understand this and expect to earn long-term average returns consistently on a short-term basis.

SEP retirement plan – A tax-advantaged retirement savings plan frequently used by sole proprietors and small businesses.

Statistical Prediction Methodology – An empirical rules-based method of making decisions designed to minimize human error.

Endnotes

1 DALBAR Mutual Fund Study 2007.

2 *The Little Book of Common Sense Investing*, John Bogle, pages 53 and 54.

3 Mikhail Tal, *The Life and Games of Mikhail Tal,* page 312.

4 *New in Chess,* 2007 issue #8, page 21.

5 Paul Meehl, "Causes and Effects of My Disturbing Little Book," *Journal of Personality Assessment,* 1986.

6 Paul Meehl, *Clinical versus Statistical Prediction,* page 5.

7 J. Sawyer, "Measurement and Prediction, Clinical versus Statistical Judgment," *Psychological Bulletin,* 1966.

8 Robyn Dawes, *Journal of Clinical Psychology.*

9 Robyn Dawes, *House of Cards,* pages 87–89.

10 Ian Ayres, *Super Crunchers: Why Thinking by the Numbers Is the New Way to Be Smart,* pages 104–108.

11 Malcolm Gladwell, *Blink: The Power of Thinking without Thinking.*

12 *The Journal of Consulting Psychology* 29 (1965), pages 261–265.

13 Nassim Nicholas Taleb, *The Black Swan,* page 158.

14 Ibid.

15 United States Equity Research, Salomon Brothers, December 1995.

16 Jerome Groopman, MD, *How Doctors Think,* pages 48–53.

17 *Smart Money,* March of 2000.

18 Taleb, page 161.

19 David Faust, *The Limits of Scientific Reasoning,* page 61.

[20] Ibid, page 63.

[21] It is a simple math calculation. In fifteen years there are thirteen three-year periods. Years 1–3 are the first period; years 2–4 are the next, etc. The probability that over a given three-year period our hypothetical manager will underperform the market is $.4 \times .4 \times .4$, or 6.4 percent. So the probability of not having three consecutive years of underperformance is 93.6 percent. The calculation is $(.936)^{13} = .4232$. Since there is a 42 percent chance that the manager will not have three or more down years, we know there is a 58 percent chance that the manager will experience three or more years of underperformance.

[22] To calculate this, remember that in fifteen years there are twelve separate four-year periods (years 1–4, years 2–5, etc.). So the probability that our star manager underperforms in any one of those twelve four-year periods is $1-[1-(.4)^4]^{12} = 27$ percent.

[23] This calculation is a relatively simple application of probability theory. For our manager to underperform, he must do worse than the market more years than he beats it. So the probability he underperforms is the sum of the chance that he trails eight years and beats the market seven years plus the chance he trails nine years and beats the market six years plus the chance he trails ten years and beats the market five years, etc. The probability he trails eight years and beats the market seven years is $(.6)^7 \times (.4)^8 \times (15!/(8! \times 7!) = 11.8056$ percent. The probability he beats the market six times and trails nine times is 6.1214 percent. The probability he beats the market only five times is 2.4486 percent. Summing these probabilities gives one the chance that our star manager trails after fifteen years.

[24] Faust, page 70.

[25] It is really a very simple problem if you remember your high school geometry, specifically the Pythagorean theorem. The distance the round travels in the air forms the hypotenuse of a right triangle. The ground distances covered in one second are 1,905 feet, 1,556 feet, and 1,100 feet, respectively.

[26] Thomas Gilovich, *How We Know What Isn't So,* page 33.

[27] Your hypothesis is if there is a vowel on one side of the card, there is an even number on the opposite side. Most people turn over the *A* card and the *2* card. They turn these cards over looking for confirmation of the hypothesis. But the *2* card is irrelevant. If there is a consonant on the other side of the *2* card, it does not disprove the hypothesis. The cards that must be turned over are the *A* card and the *3* card. These are the only cards that can disprove the hypothesis.

[28] Taleb, page 58.

[29] If you guess the next three numbers are 20, 22, and 24, the researcher will say that you are correct. But the rule is not adding two to the next number. You need to try *disconfirmation* strategies. For your next guess, try adding three to the last number and guess 21, 24, and 27, for example. The researcher will say this guess is also correct. By using disconfirmation strategies, you have a much better chance to accurately guess the rule. In fact, the rule was simple: place numbers in sequential order from lowest to highest.

[30] Joel Greenblatt, *The Little Book That Beats the Market.*

[31] Ken Fisher, *The Only Three Questions That Count,* page 126.

[32] Peter Lynch, *One Up on Wall Street,* page 65.

[33] Michael Lewis, *Moneyball,* chapters 2–4.

[34] *60 Minutes,* aired Sunday, March 30, 2008.

[35] Provided by Stephanie Ptak, courtesy of DALBAR, Inc.

[36] John C. Bogle, *The Little Book of Common Sense Investing,* page 56.

[37] *Stifel Nicolaus Equity Compass,* December 2005.

[38] Stifel Nicolaus equity presentation, February 2008.

[39] Richard Cripps, private conversation with author, March 26, 2008.

[40] White paper prepared by Jeremy J. Siegel, Luciano Siracusano, and Jeremy D. Schwartz.

[41] Greenblatt, page 56.

[42] Ibid, page 61.

[43] Ibid, page 64.

[44] A company with a price-to-sales ratio of .5 has revenues that are twice its stock price. So if a company's share price is $20 and it has $1 per share in earnings, we know it has $40 per share in sales and net profit margins of 2.5 percent. We can calculate the net profit margin by dividing the $1 of earnings by the $40 per share in revenue. If a company can increase its margins from 2.5 percent to 7.5 percent without increasing its sales, it can increase its earnings to $3 per share, and the stock price may respond in a very positive way.

[45] Ken Fisher, *Super Stocks,* pages 171–193.

[46] James O'Shaughnessy, *Predicting the Markets of Tomorrow,* page 165.

[47] James O'Shaughnessy, *What Works on Wall Street,* page 3.

[48] JPMorgan Market Insight Series, 1Q09.

[49] *Barron's,* December 22, 2008, "What We Wrote about Madoff."

[50] Henry Blodget, clusterstock.alleyinsider.com, December 23, 2008.

[51] *Barron's,* "What We Wrote about Madoff."

[52] *Herald Sun,* January 22, 2009, "Bernard Madoff: Chaos Still Emerging."

Additional Readings

I read a lot of books in preparation for writing *The Naked Portfolio Manager*. There were some excellent books, which I did not cite, that influenced the development of the theory. There are some books referenced in the text that I cannot recommend reading because they are excessively complicated or difficult to read. The books listed below are both readable and interesting.

Books on Using Math to Solve Problems

I highly recommend *Super Crunchers* by Ian Ayers. Ayers is a professor at Yale with a law degree and a degree in econometrics. In this easy-to-read book, he explains how algorithms play a huge role in our lives and can influence things such as what movies we watch and what books we read and even the people we marry. It sounds crazy, but algorithmic programs analyze your past decisions regarding the movies you rent from Netflix and the books you purchase from Amazon and suggest appropriate movies and books for your consideration in the future. Internet dating services are matching people based on numbers. Ayers shows why algorithms frequently result in better decisions than human judgment.

Fortune's Formula is by William Poundstone, an excellent writer who has twice been nominated for a Pulitzer prize. This book is a fascinating account of the Kelly formula, a mathematical formula that was used to beat Las Vegas casinos and has been applied in a host of investment scenarios. The book graphically illustrates the difference between risk and uncertainty, telling the story of Ed Thorpe, a math genius who wrote the first book about a card-counting system that turned the casinos on their heads. While Thorpe could count cards and assess the risk/reward ratio at the blackjack table, he couldn't accurately assess the chance he would be blackballed from the casino, arrested for cheating, or roughed up by the casino bosses.

Moneyball by Michael Lewis is a must-read for anyone interested in mathematics or baseball. Lewis tells the story of the seasoned baseball scout whose eye for identifying good baseball prospects just can't win as many ball games as the number-crunching statistician. He explains how Billy Beane and the Oakland A's are consistently able to win more games than larger market teams with much bigger budgets for acquiring players by carefully identifying inefficiencies in the market for baseball players.

Although *The Black Swan* by Nassim Nicholas Taleb is a difficult read, I still recommend it. The title of the book is a metaphor for an extremely unlikely event. While all of us have seen white swans, few of us have seen black swans. Therefore, he poses the question, "How many white swans must one see to conclude that there are no black swans?" Taleb explains why extremely unlikely events happen much more frequently than people expect. He shows us when we can rely on experts' opinions and when we should choose another way to make a decision.

Clinical vs. Statistical Prediction by Paul Meehl is a wonderful book for those fascinated by decision theory. Meehl wrote this book in his early thirties, and it is very interesting to compare this work to his later writings. This book is a kind of "Where's the beef?" book, suggesting that if the clinician were superior at prediction, studies should bear this out. He confesses that he can't find evidence to support the superiority of the clinician and opines that much of the work clinicians do would be more cost effectively done by clerical people using SPMs. Later in life he wrote much more authoritatively, suggesting it was high time to recognize the value of statistical prediction.

BOOKS ON PSYCHOLOGY

House of Cards: Psychology and Psychotherapy Built on Myth by Robyn Dawes is a fascinating read. Dawes carps at psychological theories that seem more designed to enrich the psychologists than to benefit the patient. He rails against expert witnesses used in litigation who make statements such as "based on my experience" when there is no evidence that their experience is useful for making predictions.

The Limits of Scientific Reasoning by Davis Faust is an extremely important book. Faust explains why judgment is so frequently flawed. What I really like is that the book gives a framework for determining which decisions should be delegated to statistical prediction, and gives useful advice for improving human judgment.

BOOKS ON THINKING

How Doctors Think by Jerome Groopman, MD, is an easy and enjoyable read. Although the title is about physicians, the principles apply to anyone making professional-level decisions under uncertain conditions. It demonstrates that doctors make many of the same types of thinking errors discussed in *The Naked Portfolio Manager*. There is a fascinating story in the book about the author's experiences as a patient and how he interacted with other physicians before they realized he and his spouse were medical doctors. Reading the book will not just give you insights into thinking errors, but will also make you a more intelligent consumer of health-care services.

The Seven Deadly Chess Sins by Grandmaster Jonathan Rowson is a wonderful book about how human nature prevents us from performing optimally on the chessboard. Rowson's key point is that mistakes on the chessboard have a commonality, and we continue to make the same types of mistakes over and over because of deficiencies in our thought processes.

Six Thinking Hats by Edward De Bono is a short, little book that can help you think better. It is a very practical book with strategies for exploring new approaches to problem solving.

Books on Confirmation Bias

The Only Three Questions That Count: Investing by Knowing What Others Don't by Ken Fisher is an entire book devoted to disconfirmation strategies, although he does not use this term. Fisher makes the point that beating the market is not a craft that can be taught in school, so to beat the market, you need an edge. The first of his three questions is, "What do I believe that is false?" His point is that if you believe something is true about investing, it is likely that many other people also believe it to be true. If it turns out not to be true, it can give you an edge in investing.

How We Know What Isn't So by Thomas Gilovich is an easy-to-read book that presents examples of disastrous reasoning in everyday life and explains the cognitive reasons for these errors. People used to think that the world was flat and that the earth was the center of the universe. After you read this book, you will be asking yourself what beliefs you have that are not true.

Books on the Stock Market

Contrarian Investment Strategies: The Next Generation by David Dreman is an extremely well-written, well-researched book that discusses how to take advantage of psychological errors in the marketplace. Investors looking to create their own rules for investing will find much of value here.

One Up on Wall Street by Peter Lynch discusses some of the advantages individual investors have over fund managers. Despite the fact that he became famous as a mutual fund manager, Lynch clearly believes that intelligent investors should consider buying individual equities.

Index

www.theNakedPortfolioManager.com